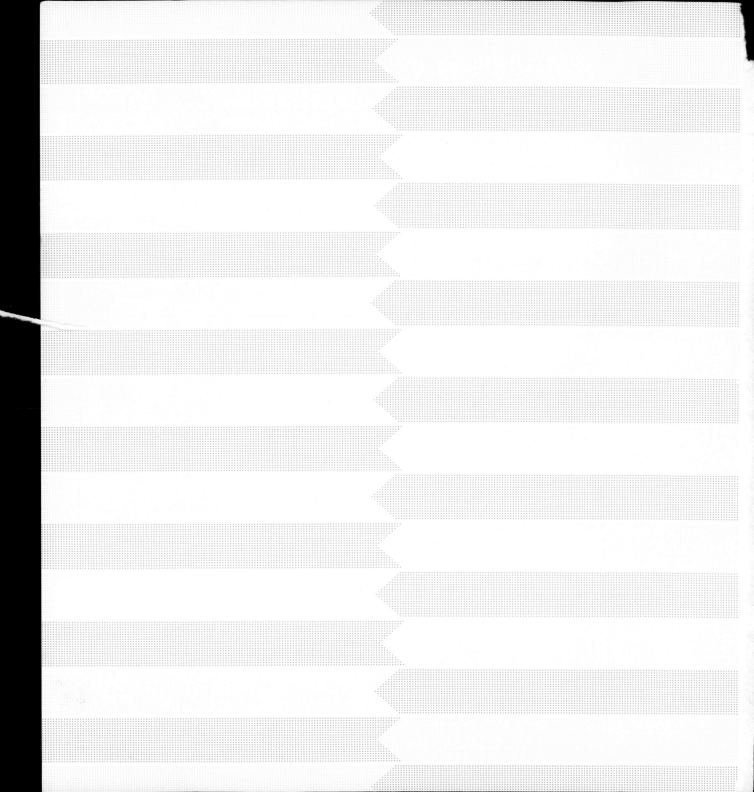

Cake Magic!

MIX & MATCH
YOUR WAY TO 100
AMAZING COMBINATIONS

CAROLINE WRIGHT

WORKMAN PUBLISHING ★ NEW YORK

Published simultaneously in Canada by Thomas Allen & Son Limited.

Library of Congress Cataloging-in-Publication Data is available.

ISBN 978-0-7611-8203-0

Interior design by Galen Smith
Cover design by Becky Terhune

Cover photo and interior photos by Waterbury Publications, Inc.,
    Des Moines, IA
Ken Carlson, Photographer
Jennifer Peterson, Contributing Food Stylist
Photo, page vi, by Manny Rodriguez
Napkin background on back cover ©Mayakova/Fotolia

Workman books are available at special discounts when purchased in bulk for premiums and sales promotions as well as for fund-raising or educational use. Special editions or book excerpts also can be created to specification. For details, contact the Special Sales Director at the address below, or send an email to specialmarkets@workman.com.

Workman Publishing Company, Inc.
225 Varick Street
New York, NY 10014-4381
workman.com

WORKMAN is a registered trademark of Workman Publishing Co., Inc.

Printed in China

First printing May 2016

DEDICATION

For Henry, whose fifth word was "cake."

ACKNOWLEDGMENTS

Many thanks to my husband, Garth, for lending his seemingly endless supply of time, energy, and taste buds to this project. A very special thanks, too, to Katie Wilson for her diligent recipe testing.

CONTENTS

INTRODUCTION

My friends will tell you that I am among the sneakiest of cake bakers. Months before a pal's birthday, I will surreptitiously ply him or her with questions (and often wine) to suss out his or her favorite cake. Later, on the big day, I'll smuggle a freshly baked cake into a crowded bar, tuck one under my arm on the subway, or leave one on a doorstep—whatever it takes to deliver a surprise gift to a wide-eyed friend who only vaguely recalls our conversation from six months earlier.

My sleuthing is born of the belief that there's magic in baking someone a perfect cake, doubly so if it's a new favorite, made even better with an unexpected twist. It is that magic—and the joy of giving a gift in cake form—that I hope to share with you in this book.

What you'll find in these pages are simple, dependable, *fun* recipes for cakes that are as inspiring to bake as they are to share. Each one begins with an easy, from-scratch mix that forms the foundation of a range of delectable batters, from vanilla to chocolate, citrus to coconut, and everything in between. Pour a simple flavored syrup (the professional baker's secret weapon!) over the still-warm cake layers, add one of a dozen dead-easy frostings, maybe a quick topping or two—and you've got a hundred cake possibilities. The cake's destination is up to you—I've just handed you some great reasons to make the trip.

Cake—even just the promise of it—brings people together. Browse through the pages that follow and get ready to join the legion of cake bakers whose celebrations start in the kitchen. I am so happy to have you here, and hope that you'll find your next favorite cake lurking among these recipes.

Caroline

HOW TO USE THIS BOOK

Ready to roll up those sleeves, raid your pantry, and start mixing up a cake? Great! But before you jump in, permit me to give you a quick preview of how this book works.

The bulk of the pages feature not recipes, but equations: Each one shows a picture of a cake and directs you to the components—a batter + a syrup + a frosting + (sometimes) a topping—used to make it spectacular. This book has more photos than recipes to illustrate the versatility of the simple, basic anatomy of the cakes. The recipes are almost instinctual and will soon become second nature: Bake and assemble one cake, and you'll know how it works for all one hundred. The process for each cake is essentially the same—only the flavors change. Here is the basic breakdown:

1. Flip to the photo of a cake you want to make. Drool. Note the page references for the cake batter, flavoring syrup, and frosting recipes needed to make it.

2. Turn to the back of the book to find the recipes. Mark each with one of the colored ribbons.

3. Make a batch of Cake Magic! Cake Mix (page 142), which serves as the foundation for every cake in the book.

....

4. Follow the recipes you've marked—you'll be making cake layers, a flavored syrup, frosting, and so on—and assemble the cake as directed on page 120.

....

5. Eat!

A NOTE FOR GLUTEN-FREE AND VEGAN BAKERS AND EATERS:
I want everyone to feel comfortable playing around in the kitchen, and even breaking a few baking rules. When I say "everyone," I'm including people with food restrictions for whom cake baking (and eating) can be challenging. With them in mind, I've created a Gluten-Free Cake Magic! Cake Mix (page 143) that works as a substitute for the one using all-purpose flour. For vegan bakers, I've offered variations on the batters that make any cake in this book vegan-friendly. (And any recipes that are already gluten-free or vegan are marked accordingly with these respective icons: **GF** • **V**.) These variations are supremely tasty and were developed to mimic the texture and flavors of the cakes made with all the standard components. They can be syruped, frosted, topped, and—best of all—enjoyed just like any other cake in this book.

These recipes work as cupcakes, Bundts, and sheet cakes, too—for instructions on adapting them, see pages 120–121.

Vanilla Cakes

Sprinkle cake with rainbow sprinkles and/or nonpareils.

Confetti Cake (PAGE 144)   **+**   **Vanilla Syrup** (PAGE 152)   **+**   **Malted Vanilla Frosting** (PAGE 163)   **=**   CONFETTI CAKE

Sprinkle Shortbread Crumble (page 179) between layers and on top.

Vanilla Cake
(PAGE 144) **+** **Sweet Cream Syrup** (PAGE 153) **+** **Malted Vanilla Frosting** (PAGE 163) **=** SWEET CREAM CAKE

Sprinkle Chocolate Cookie Crumble (page 179) on top (and between layers for a layer cake).

①

Garnish with fresh blackberries and/or dust with confectioners' sugar.

②

Vanilla Cake (PAGE 144) + **Sweet Cream Syrup** (PAGE 153) + **Malted Vanilla Frosting** (PAGE 163) = **COOKIES + CREAM CAKE** ①

Reserve about ½ cup Salted Caramel and swirl into the frosting (see page 137). Sprinkle with sliced almonds.

③

②

③

Buttermilk Cake (PAGE 144)	+	Blackberry Syrup (PAGE 154)	+	Cream Cheese Frosting (PAGE 164)	=	BLACKBERRY BUTTERMILK CAKE
Vanilla-Cinnamon Cake (PAGE 144)	+	Sweet Cream Syrup (PAGE 153)	+	Salted Caramel Frosting (PAGE 165)	=	HORCHATA + CARAMEL CAKE

Spread 1 cup cherry jam or preserves between layers and garnish with fresh cherries. (If making a non-layer cake, warm the jam and spoon it over the frosted cake.)

Vanilla Cake
(PAGE 144)
+
Cherry Syrup
(PAGE 154)
+
Bittersweet Chocolate Frosting
(PAGE 166)
=
VANILLA, CHERRY + CHOCOLATE CAKE

Pineapple Upside-Down Cake (PAGE 144) + **Rum Syrup** (PAGE 155) + **Salted Caramel Frosting** (PAGE 165) = CARAMEL PINEAPPLE UPSIDE-DOWN CAKE

Vanilla Cake
(PAGE 144)

+

Milky Caramel Syrup
(PAGE 153)

+

Salted Caramel Frosting
(PAGE 165)

=

CREAMY CARAMEL CAKE

Reserve ½ cup Salted Caramel and swirl into the frosting (see page 137).

Top with Pecans in Syrup (page 177), if you like.

| Vanilla Cake (PAGE 144) | + | Buttered Rum Syrup (PAGE 155) | + | Bittersweet Chocolate Frosting (PAGE 166) | = | BUTTERED RUM CAKE WITH CHOCOLATE FROSTING |

Scatter about 2 cups fresh mixed berries between layers and on top.

| Vanilla Cake | | Bourbon-Berry Syrup | | Malted Vanilla Frosting | | BOOZY BERRY |
| (PAGE 144) | + | (PAGE 154) | + | (PAGE 163) | = | CAKE |

*Top with
sprinkles.*

Happ
B

Vanilla Cake
(PAGE 144)

+

Vanilla Syrup
(PAGE 152)

+

**Bittersweet
Chocolate
Frosting**
(PAGE 166)

=

CLASSIC
BIRTHDAY
CAKE

Place Sautéed Apples (page 174) between layers, and swirl about 2 tablespoons apple butter on top.

Vanilla Cake (PAGE 144) **+** **Apple-Cinnamon Syrup** (PAGE 156) **+** **Cream Cheese Frosting** (PAGE 164) **=** SPICY CINNAMON CAKE WITH APPLES

Vanilla Cake
(PAGE 144) + **Milky Vodka Syrup** (PAGE 153) + **Malted Vanilla Frosting** (PAGE 163) = WHITE RUSSIAN CAKE

Sprinkle with Rosemary Sugar (page 180) and garnish with Sugared Rosemary (page 157).

Vanilla–Olive Oil Cake (PAGE 144) + **Fresh Rosemary Syrup** (PAGE 157) + **Lemon Pudding Frosting** (PAGE 167) = **VANILLA-OLIVE OIL CAKE WITH ROSEMARY + LEMON**

Garnish with about 1 cup thinly sliced fresh peaches tossed with warmed apricot jam (for a layer cake, omit the jam and place the peaches between layers).

Vanilla Cake (PAGE 144) **+** **Peach Syrup** (PAGE 154) **+** **Cream Cheese Frosting** (PAGE 164) **=** PEACHES + CREAM CAKE

Chocolate Cakes

Garnish with a drizzle of Bittersweet Chocolate Glaze (page 178), if you like.

| **Darkest Chocolate Cake** (PAGE 145) | + | **Chocolate Syrup** (PAGE 152) | + | **Bittersweet Chocolate Frosting** (PAGE 166) | = | BEST BLACKOUT CAKE |

Sprinkle Gingersnap Crumble (page 179) between layers and on top. Garnish with a drizzle of honey.

Darkest Chocolate Cake (PAGE 145)   +   **Cinnamon-Ginger Syrup** (PAGE 158)   +   **Honey Frosting** (PAGE 168)   =   WARM CHOCOLATE GINGERBREAD CAKE

Sprinkle chopped candy bars on top (and between layers for a layer cake).

| **Darkest Chocolate Cake** (PAGE 145) | + | **Milky Caramel Syrup** (PAGE 153) | + | **Malted Milk Chocolate Frosting** (PAGE 169) | = | CANDY BAR CAKE |

Dust the top with confectioners' sugar, if you like.

Darkest Chocolate Cake (PAGE 145) **+** **Tea Syrup** (PAGE 159) **+** **Lemon Pudding Frosting** (PAGE 167) **=** CHOCOLATE CAKE WITH TEA + LEMON

Sprinkle chopped chocolate mint cookies, such as Thin Mints, between layers and on top. Garnish with fresh mint leaves.

Darkest Chocolate Cake (PAGE 145) **+** **Fresh Mint Syrup** (PAGE 157) **+** **Bittersweet Chocolate Frosting** (PAGE 166) **=** GRASSHOPPER CAKE

Top with shaved chocolate (see page 178).

Darkest Chocolate Cake (PAGE 145) + **Bourbon Syrup** (PAGE 155) + **Cream Cheese Frosting** (PAGE 164) = **DRUNKEN TUXEDO CAKE**

Sprinkle with flaked sea salt.

①

Darkest Chocolate Cake (PAGE 145)	+	**Vanilla Syrup** (PAGE 152)	+	**Salted Caramel Frosting** (PAGE 165)	= SALTED CARAMEL CHOCOLATE CAKE ①
Darkest Chocolate Cake (PAGE 14)	+	**Fresh Basil Syrup** (PAGE 157)	+	**Salted Caramel Frosting** (PAGE 165)	= DARK CHOCOLATE CAKE WITH BASIL + CARAMEL ②

Sprinkle Basil Sugar (page 180) on top.

②

Garnish with orange zest.

③

Darkest Chocolate Cake (PAGE 145) + **Orange Syrup** (PAGE 159) + **Salted Caramel Frosting** (PAGE 165) = **CHOCOLATE-ORANGE CAKE WITH CARAMEL FROSTING** ③

Garnish with Hazelnuts in Syrup (page 172). If making a Bundt cake, use the sheet cake frosting variation or the glaze variation on page 162.

Darkest Chocolate Cake
(PAGE 145)

+

Milky Cocoa Syrup
(PAGE 153)

+

Nutella Frosting
(PAGE 162)

=

CHOCOLATE-HAZELNUT CAKE

Use about 3 cups flaked or shredded coconut to coat the cake and sprinkle between layers.

Darkest Chocolate Cake + Coconut Syrup + Malted Vanilla Frosting = HOSTESS CAKE
(PAGE 145)   (PAGE 160)   (PAGE 163)

Reserve a couple of spoonfuls of Spiced Red Wine Syrup to drizzle on top.

| **Darkest Chocolate Cake** (PAGE 145) | + | **Spiced Red Wine Syrup** (PAGE 158) | + | **Bittersweet Chocolate Frosting** (PAGE 166) | = | CHOCOLATE + RED WINE CAKE |

Reserve a couple spoonfuls Cola Syrup to drizzle on top or serve alongside.

Darkest Chocolate Cola Cake (PAGE 145) **+** **Cola Syrup** (PAGE 156) **+** **Malted Vanilla Frosting** (PAGE 163) **=** SODA FOUNTAIN CAKE

Sprinkle toasted sliced or chopped almonds (page 176) on top.

Darkest Chocolate Cake (PAGE 145) + **Sweet and Smoky Chile Syrup** (PAGE 158) + **Malted Milk Chocolate Frosting** (PAGE 169) = **SPICY HOT CHOCOLATE CAKE**

Dust the top with finely grated chocolate. Sandwich layers with Sautéed Pears (page 174).

Darkest Chocolate Cake (PAGE 145) **+** **Pear Syrup** (PAGE 154) **+** **Cream Cheese Frosting** (PAGE 164) **=** CHOCOLATE + PEAR CAKE

Citrus Cakes

Swirl about 1 cup crushed fresh berries into the frosting (see page 137).

Lemon Cake (PAGE 146) **+** **Mixed Berry Syrup** (PAGE 154) **+** **Malted Vanilla Frosting** (PAGE 163) **=** SUMMER LEMON CAKE ①

③

Reserve ½ cup Tea
Syrup to drizzle on
top. Garnish with
lemon zest.

②

Swirl ½ cup blueberry jam
into the frosting (see
page 137).

| Lemon-Ricotta Cake (PAGE 146) | + | Blueberry Syrup (PAGE 154) | + | Cream Cheese Frosting (PAGE 164) | = | BLUEBERRY LEMON-RICOTTA CAKE | ② |

| Lemon Cake (PAGE 146) | + | Tea Syrup (PAGE 159) | + | Malted Vanilla Frosting (PAGE 163) | = | ARNOLD PALMER CAKE | ③ |

Spread 1 cup orange
marmalade between
layers and swirl ½ cup
into frosting (see page
137). Garnish with
orange zest.

Orange Cake
(PAGE 146)
+
**Cardamom
Syrup**
(PAGE 158)
+
**Honey
Frosting**
(PAGE 168)
=
ORANGE + CARDAMOM
CAKE WITH HONEY
FROSTING

Garnish with about 2 cups hulled fresh strawberries tossed in warmed apricot jam.

Lemon Cake (PAGE 146) + **Strawberry Syrup** (PAGE 154) + **Strawberry Frosting** (PAGE 170) = **STRAWBERRY-LEMON CAKE**

Lemon Cake
(PAGE 146) **+** **Lemon Syrup**
(PAGE 159) **+** **Lemon Pudding Frosting**
(PAGE 167) **=** LEMON PUCKER CAKE

Sprinkle Shortbread Crumble *(page 179)* between layers and on top.

Lemon–Poppy Seed Cake (PAGE 146) **+** **Tea Syrup** (PAGE 159) **+** **Lemon Pudding Frosting** (PAGE 167) **=** HIGH TEA CAKE

Place Caramelized Grapefruit (page 175) between layers and on top.

Grapefruit Cake
(PAGE 146)

\+

Cinnamon Syrup
(PAGE 158)

\+

Cream Cheese Frosting
(PAGE 164)

\=

SPICED GRAPEFRUIT + CREAM CAKE

Garnish with orange, lemon, and lime zest.

Lime Cake
(PAGE 146) **+** **Orange Syrup**
(PAGE 159) **+** **Lemon Pudding Frosting**
(PAGE 167) **=** TRIPLE CITRUS CAKE

Garnish with lemon zest and finely chopped crystallized ginger.

Lemon Cake (PAGE 146) **+** **Ginger Syrup** (PAGE 158) **+** **Bittersweet Chocolate Frosting** (PAGE 166) **=** **LEMON-GINGER CAKE WITH CHOCOLATE FROSTING**

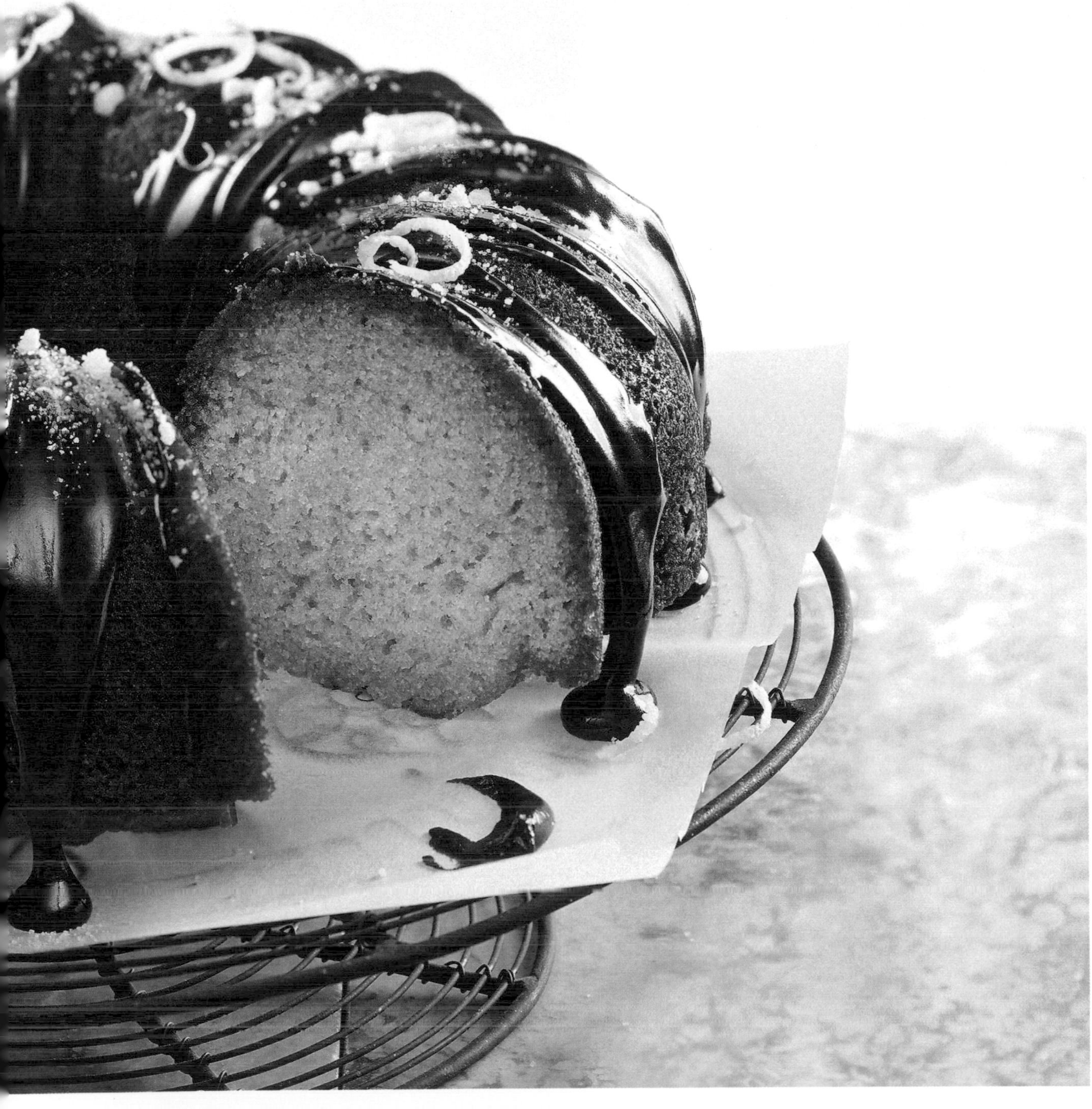

Spread 1 cup Lemon Pudding (page 173) or store-bought lemon curd between the layers. Drizzle slices with honey, if you like.

Lemon Cake (PAGE 146) + **Buttered Rum Syrup** (PAGE 155) + **Honey Frosting** (PAGE 168) = HOT TODDY'S LEMON CAKE

Sprinkle Basil Sugar (page 180) on top.

Lemon Cake
(PAGE 146)

+

Fresh Basil Syrup
(PAGE 157)

+

Cream Cheese Frosting
(PAGE 164)

=

BASIL + LEMON
CREAM CAKE

Brown Sugar Cakes *

Garnish with fresh cherries.

Brown Sugar–
Nut Cake
(PAGE 147)

+

Cherry
Syrup
(PAGE 154)

+

Cream Cheese
Frosting
(PAGE 164)

=

SOUTHERN
DINER CAKE

Swirl ½ cup store-bought cookie butter (aka Speculoos) into frosting (see page 137). Sprinkle Shortbread Crumble (page 179) between layers and on top.

Brown Sugar Cake (PAGE 147) + **Spiced Syrup** (PAGE 158) + **Cookie-Butter Frosting** (PAGE 163) = COOKIE-BUTTER CAKE

Garnish sides with chocolate chips.

Chocolate Chip Cookie Cake (PAGE 147) + **Sweet Cream Syrup** (PAGE 153) + **Malted Vanilla Frosting** (PAGE 163) = **CHOCOLATE CHIP COOKIE CAKE**

*Top with Candied
Bacon (page 161).*

**Brown Sugar
Cake**
(PAGE 147)   **+**   **Bacon-Maple
Syrup**
(PAGE 161)   **+**   **Bittersweet
Chocolate
Frosting**
(PAGE 166)   **=**   MAPLE, BACON
+ CHOCOLATE
CAKE

*Sprinkle Graham
Cracker Crumble
(page 179) between
layers and on
sides. Garnish
with Toasted
Marshmallows
(page 177).*

| Brown Sugar Cake (PAGE 147) | + | Vanilla Syrup (PAGE 152) | + | Bittersweet Chocolate Frosting (PAGE 166) | = | S'MORES CAKE |

Sprinkle with toasted, chopped walnuts (page 176).

Brown Sugar–Nut Cake (PAGE 147) + Ginger Syrup (PAGE 158) + Honey Frosting (PAGE 168) = HONEY-WALNUT CAKE WITH GINGER SYRUP

Root Beer
Cake
(PAGE 147)

+

Root Beer
Syrup
(PAGE 156)

+

Malted Vanilla
Frosting
(PAGE 163)

=

ROOT BEER
FLOAT CAKE

**Brown Sugar–
Cinnamon
Raisin Cake**
(PAGE 147)

+

**Buttered
Rum Syrup**
(PAGE 155)

+

**Malted Vanilla
Frosting**
(PAGE 163)

=

RUM RAISIN
CAKE

Sprinkle with Sandy Cinnamon Sugar (page 180).

Brown Sugar–Cinnamon Cake (PAGE 147) **+** Cinnamon Syrup (PAGE 158) **+** Bittersweet Chocolate Frosting (PAGE 166) **=** CINNAMON-SUGAR CAKE WITH CHOCOLATE FROSTING

Reserve about ½ cup Salted Caramel and swirl into the frosting (see page 137).

Brown Sugar Cake (PAGE 147) + **Buttered Scotch Syrup** (PAGE 155) + **Salted Caramel Frosting** (PAGE 165) = BUTTERSCOTCH CAKE

*Garnish with Pecans
in Syrup (page 177).*

Brown Sugar
Cake
(PAGE 147)

+

Spiced Maple
Syrup
(PAGE 158)

+

Cream Cheese
Frosting
(PAGE 164)

=

PECAN BUN
CAKE

①

Sprinkle top of cake with
Oat Streusel (page 179).

Sprinkle with toasted pine
nuts or sliced almonds
(page 176).

(3)

Brown Sugar Cake	+	Maple Syrup	+	Malted Vanilla Frosting	=	MAPLE VANILLA BRUNCH CAKE	(2)
(PAGE 147)		(PAGE 152)		(PAGE 163)			
Browned Butter Cake	+	Spiced Syrup	+	Malted Vanilla Frosting	=	BROWNED BUTTER CAKE	(3)
(PAGE 147)		(PAGE 158)		(PAGE 163)			

Sprinkle chopped toffee bars, such as Heath Bars, between layers and on top.

Brown Sugar Cake	+	Milky Caramel Syrup	+	Malted Milk Chocolate Frosting	=	TOFFEE CAKE
(PAGE 147)		(PAGE 153)		(PAGE 169)		

Spread 1 cup Lemon Pudding (page 173) or store-bought lemon curd between layers. Garnish with lemon zest.

Earl Grey

| Brown Sugar Cake (PAGE 147) | + | Tea Syrup (PAGE 159) | + | Cream Cheese Frosting (PAGE 164) | = | TEA WITH CREAM + SUGAR CAKE |

fruit + Veggie Cakes

Coat sides of cake with Toasted Coconut (page 176).

Carrot Cake (PAGE 148) **+** **Coconut Syrup** (PAGE 160) **+** **Cream Cheese Frosting** (PAGE 164) **=** CARROT + COCONUT CAKE

Reserve ½ cup Maple Syrup (page 152) and drizzle over top.

Banana Cake (PAGE 148) **+** **Maple Syrup** (PAGE 152) **+** **Malted Vanilla Frosting** (PAGE 163) **=** BANANA-MAPLE CAKE + MALTED VANILLA FROSTING

Garnish with Walnuts in Syrup (page 177).

Apple Cake (PAGE 148)	**+** **Spiced Syrup** (PAGE 158)	**+** **Honey Frosting** (PAGE 168)	**=**	FALL HARVEST CAKE ①
Apple Cider Cake (PAGE 148)	**+** **Cider Syrup** (PAGE 156)	**+** **Malted Vanilla Frosting** (PAGE 163)	**=**	APPLE CIDER CAKE ②

③

②

Swirl about ½ cup apple butter on top of frosted cake.

Pumpkin Cake
(PAGE 148)

+

Spiced Syrup
(PAGE 158)

+

Bittersweet Chocolate Frosting
(PAGE 166)

=

PUMPKIN-
CHOCOLATE
CAKE

③

Sprinkle with Thyme Sugar (page 180).

Zucchini Cake (PAGE 148) + **Fresh Thyme Syrup** (PAGE 157) + **Lemon Pudding Frosting** (PAGE 167) = ZUCCHINI-THYME CAKE WITH LEMON PUDDING FROSTING

Garnish with crumbled ginger snaps.

Pumpkin Cake (PAGE 148)   **+**   **Ginger Syrup** (PAGE 158)   **+**   **Cream Cheese Frosting** (PAGE 164)   **=**   **PUMPKIN-GINGER CAKE WITH CREAM CHEESE FROSTING**

Garnish top with fresh blueberries tossed with warmed apricot jam.

Fresh Blueberry Cake (PAGE 148) + **Vanilla Syrup** (PAGE 152) + **Cream Cheese Frosting** (PAGE 164) = **FRESH BLUEBERRY CAKE**

Garnish with shaved chocolate (see page 178).

| Pear Cake (PAGE 148) | + | Cinnamon Syrup (PAGE 158) | + | Bittersweet Chocolate Frosting (PAGE 166) | = | PEAR CAKE WITH CHOCOLATE FROSTING |

Swirl about ½ cup pear butter or apple butter on top of the frosted cake.

Pear Cake (PAGE 148) **+** **Spiced Syrup** (PAGE 158) **+** **Honey Frosting** (PAGE 168) **=** CHAI-PEAR CAKE WITH HONEY FROSTING

Apple Cake
(PAGE 148)   **+**   **Milky Caramel Syrup**
(PAGE 153)   **+**   **Salted Caramel Frosting**
(PAGE 165)   **=**   CARAMEL APPLE CAKE

Place Caramelized
Bananas (page 175)
in between layers.

Banana Cake
(PAGE 148)   **+**   **Milky Caramel Syrup**
(PAGE 153)   **+**   **Malted Milk Chocolate Frosting**
(PAGE 169)   **=**   BANANA-CARAMEL CAKE
WITH MALTED MILK
CHOCOLATE FROSTING

Top with sprinkles or lime zest.

Carrot Cake (PAGE 148) + **Lime Syrup** (PAGE 159) + **Cream Cheese Frosting** (PAGE 164) = **CARROT-LIME CAKE WITH CREAM CHEESE FROSTING**

CHAPTER 6

Nutty Cakes

Place about 1 cup fresh blackberries between layers.

Peanut Butter Cake (PAGE 149) **+** **Blackberry Syrup** (PAGE 154) **+** **Malted Vanilla Frosting** (PAGE 163) **=** **SCHOOL LUNCH CAKE**

Coat the sides of the cake with about 2 cups crushed pretzels.

Peanut Butter Cake (PAGE 149) + Milky Caramel Syrup (PAGE 153) + Salted Caramel Frosting (PAGE 165) = PEANUT BUTTER PRETZEL CAKE WITH SALTED CARAMEL FROSTING

Peanut Butter Cake
(PAGE 149)

+

Chocolate Syrup
(PAGE 152)

+

Malted Milk Chocolate Frosting
(PAGE 169)

=

PEANUT BUTTER CUP CAKE

Sprinkle chopped peanut butter cups on top.

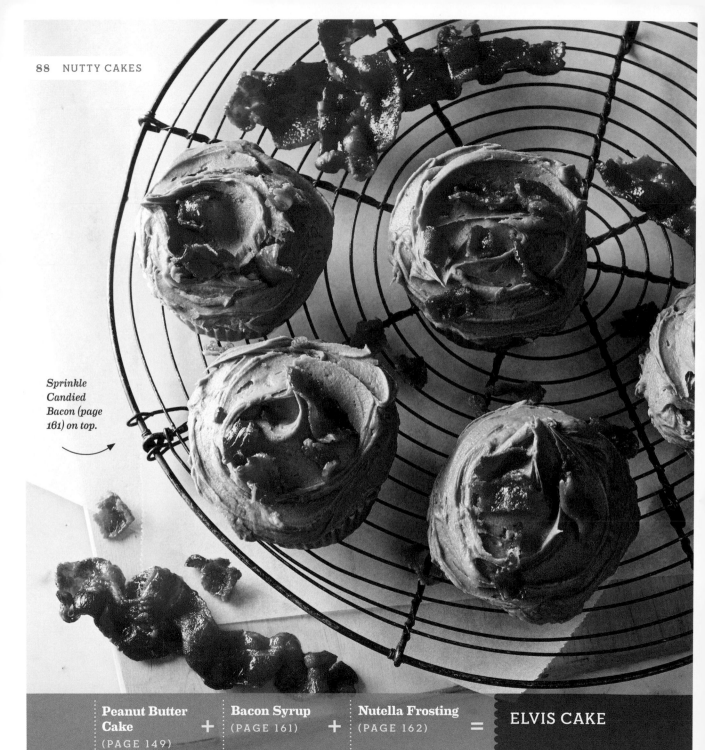

Sprinkle Candied Bacon (page 161) on top. →

Peanut Butter Cake
(PAGE 149)

+

Bacon Syrup
(PAGE 161)

+

Nutella Frosting
(PAGE 162)

=

ELVIS CAKE

Spread 1 cup apricot jam or preserves between layers. Scatter top with sliced fresh apricots tossed in warmed apricot jam.

| Cashew Butter Cake (PAGE 149) | + | Apricot-Cardamom Syrup (PAGE 158) | + | Honey Frosting (PAGE 168) | = | APRICOT, CASHEW + CARDAMOM CAKE WITH HONEY FROSTING |

Spread 1 cup orange marmalade in between layers. Top with orange zest.

②

①

| **Almond Butter Cake** (PAGE 149) | + | **Orange Syrup** (PAGE 159) | + | **Salted Caramel Frosting** (PAGE 165) | = | DINNER PARTY CAKE ① |

Dust the cake with Cinnamon Sugar (page 180).

Coat the cake with about 3 cups flaked or shredded coconut.

③

| Spiced Almond Butter Cake (PAGE 149) | + | Cinnamon Syrup (PAGE 158) | + | Honey Frosting (PAGE 168) | = | ALMOND CAKE WITH CINNAMON + HONEY | ② |
| Almond Butter Cake (PAGE 149) | + | Coconut Syrup (PAGE 160) | + | Bittersweet Chocolate Frosting (PAGE 166) | = | ALMOND JOY CAKE | ③ |

Sprinkle with finely chopped pistachios.

Pistachio Cake (PAGE 149) **+** **Spiced Syrup** (PAGE 158) **+** **Lemon Pudding Frosting** (PAGE 167) **=** PISTACHIO + LEMON CAKE

Garnish with a mound of Roasted Grapes (page 175).

| Spiced Almond Butter Cake (PAGE 149) | + | Spiced Syrup (PAGE 158) | + | Cream Cheese Frosting (PAGE 164) | = | SPICED ALMOND CAKE WITH CREAM CHEESE FROSTING |

Coconut Cakes

Sandwich 1 cup sliced fresh strawberries between layers.

Coconut Cake (PAGE 150) **+** **Strawberry Syrup** (PAGE 154) **+** **Strawberry Frosting** (PAGE 170) **=** COCONUT CAKE WITH STRAWBERRY FROSTING

*Garnish with
Toasted Coconut
(page 176).*

| Coconut
Cake
(PAGE 150) | + | Milky
Caramel
Syrup
(PAGE 153) | + | Malted Milk
Chocolate
Frosting
(PAGE 169) | = | COCONUT-CARAMEL
CAKE WITH MALTED
CHOCOLATE FROSTING |

Drizzle with melted white chocolate (see page 125).

Coconut–White Chocolate Cake		Sweet Cream Syrup		Malted Vanilla Frosting		COCONUT–WHITE CHOCOLATE CAKE
(PAGE 150)	+	(PAGE 153)	+	(PAGE 163)	=	

Sprinkle with chocolate chips, if you like.

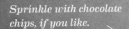

Coconut–Chocolate
Chip Cake
(PAGE 150)

+

Sweet Cream
Syrup
(PAGE 153)

+

Salted Caramel
Frosting
(PAGE 165)

=

DREAM CAKE

Sprinkle with Toasted Coconut
(page 176) and shaved chocolate
(see page 178).

Coconut Cake (PAGE 150)   **+**   **Coconut Syrup** (PAGE 160)   **+**   **Bittersweet Chocolate Frosting** (PAGE 166)   **=**   COCONUT + CHOCOLATE CAKE

Garnish with Crystallized Ginger Sugar (page 180) or finely chopped crystallized ginger.

Coconut Cake (PAGE 150) **+** **Gingery Buttered Rum Syrup** (PAGE 155) **+** **Malted Vanilla Frosting** (PAGE 163) **=** COCONUT, GINGER + RUM CAKE

Place Caramelized Mango (page 175) between layers.

Coconut Cake (PAGE 150) **+** **Mango Syrup** (PAGE 154) **+** **Salted Caramel Frosting** (PAGE 165) **=** MANGO-COCONUT CAKE WITH SALTED CARAMEL FROSTING

Garnish top with fresh raspberries and place about 1 cup between layers, if you like.

Coconut Cake (PAGE 150)	**+**	**Raspberry Syrup** (PAGE 154)	**+**	**Cream Cheese Frosting** (PAGE 164)	**=** COCONUT + RASPBERRY CAKE WITH CREAM CHEESE FROSTING ①
Spiced Coconut-Pecan Cake (PAGE 150)	**+**	**Sweet Cream Syrup** (PAGE 153)	**+**	**Cream Cheese Frosting** (PAGE 164)	**=** ITALIAN CREAM CAKE ②

②

③

Sprinkle Toasted Coconut (page 176) between layers and on top.

Coat the sides of cake in about 2 cups chopped pecans.

Coconut Cake
(PAGE 150)

+

Coconut Syrup
(PAGE 160)

+

Cream Cheese Frosting
(PAGE 164)

=

COCONUT
CLOUD CAKE

③

Mocha Cakes

Sprinkle 1 cup fresh raspberries between layers. Garnish with a drizzle of Bittersweet Chocolate Glaze (page 178) or store-bought chocolate fudge sauce.

| **Mocha Cake** (PAGE 151) | **+** | **Raspberry Syrup** (PAGE 154) | **+** | **Raspberry Frosting** (PAGE 170) | **=** | MOCHA RASPBERRY CAKE |

Reserve ½ cup Milky Caramel Syrup (page 153) to drizzle on top.

Mocha Cake (PAGE 151) + **Milky Caramel Syrup** (PAGE 153) + **Salted Caramel Frosting** (PAGE 165) = MOCHA CARAMEL CAKE

Mocha Cake
(PAGE 151)   +   **Coffee Syrup**
(PAGE 156)   +   **Bittersweet
Chocolate
Frosting**
(PAGE 166)   =   DOUBLE-SHOT
MOCHA CAKE

Swirl ½ cup orange marmalade into the frosting (see page 137).

Mocha Cake (PAGE 151) **+** **Orange Syrup** (PAGE 159) **+** **Cream Cheese Frosting** (PAGE 164) **=** ORANGE MOCHA CAKE + CREAM CHEESE FROSTING

Coat the sides or the entire cake with 2 to 3 cups finely chopped hazelnuts.

| **Mocha Cake** (PAGE 151) | + | **Amaretto Syrup** (PAGE 155) | + | **Nutella Frosting** (PAGE 162) | = | MULBERRY STREET CAKE |

Garnish with chopped chocolate-covered espresso beans.

| **Mocha Cake** (PAGE 151) | + | **Baileys Syrup** (PAGE 155) | + | **Malted Vanilla Frosting** (PAGE 163) | = | IRISH COFFEE CAKE | ① |

| **Mocha Cake** (PAGE 151) | + | **Sweet Cream Syrup** (PAGE 153) | + | **Malted Vanilla Frosting** (PAGE 163) | = | NEW ORLEANS CAFÉ AU LAIT CAKE | ② |

Dust the top with confectioners' sugar.

②

③

Dust with unsweetened cocoa powder and sprinkle Ladyfinger Crumble (page 179) on top.

Mocha Cake (PAGE 151) **+** **Chocolate Syrup** (PAGE 152) **+** **Malted Vanilla Frosting** (PAGE 163) **=** TIRAMISU CAKE ③

Dust with
*Spiced Chocolate
Sugar (page 180).*

Mocha Cake
(PAGE 151)   **+**   **Spiced Coffee
Syrup**
(PAGE 156)   **+**   **Cream Cheese
Frosting**
(PAGE 164)   **=**   SPICED COFFEE +
CREAM CAKE

Sprinkle top with chopped malted milk balls.

| **Mocha Cake** (PAGE 151) | + | **Stout Syrup** (PAGE 156) | + | **Malted Chocolate Frosting** (PAGE 169) | = | MALTED CHOCOLATE STOUT CAKE |

Putting It All Together

HOW TO ASSEMBLE A CAKE MAGIC! CAKE

THE QUINTESSENTIAL CAKE MAGIC! cake is an 8-inch, round, 2-layer cake. (To make one in a different shape or size, or with four layers instead of two, see pages 121 and 122, respectively.) Here is the basic method:

1. Bake the cakes. Make and bake the cake layers according to the recipe directions. (Be sure to whisk the dry mix before spooning and measuring it.) While the cake bakes, prepare the syrup and set it aside.

2. Syrup them. After removing the cake layers from the oven, pierce them (still in the pans) at 1-inch intervals with a skewer or paring knife. Pour or brush the syrup over the layers, dividing it evenly. Set the layers aside, in the pans, on a wire rack to cool completely. (The syrup will soak into the cakes.)

3. Make the frosting. When the cakes are cool and no longer wet to the touch, 1 to 2 hours, make the frosting according to the recipe directions, noting any substitutions or additions.

4. Frost a layer. Run a knife or an offset spatula around the edge of one of the layers to loosen it. (Turn the layers out of their pans one by one, as you frost them.) Place the layer on a cake plate with strips of waxed paper or parchment paper underneath; these will catch any drips and keep your cake plate clean. Spread the layer with about a third of the frosting on top, along with any desired additional fillings.

5. Frost the rest. Run a knife or an offset spatula around the edge of the remaining cake layer. Invert it onto the frosted layer. Frost the sides and top of the cake with the remaining frosting.

6. Add toppings. Scatter the frosted cake with any toppings, as directed.

ADAPTING THE CAKE MAGIC! METHOD TO OTHER PAN SHAPES

Making a cake sized and suited perfectly for your party is easy to do with a few tweaks to the Cake Magic! method.

For 8-inch square layer cakes and 9-inch round layer cakes: Use the same method as for 8-inch round cakes on page 120.

For cupcakes: Line 24 muffin tins with paper liners. Prepare the batter as directed; divide the batter among the muffin tins with the help of a dry measure (about ⅓ cup). Follow the baking times indicated in each recipe. Let the cupcakes cool in the tins for 10 minutes, then transfer them to a wire rack. While the cupcakes are still warm, use a skewer to pierce them all over at 1-inch intervals. Pour or brush the syrup over the cupcakes, dividing it evenly. Set the cupcakes aside to cool completely. (The syrup will soak into the cupcakes.) When the cupcakes are cool and no longer wet to the touch, about 1 hour, make the frosting according to the recipe directions and frost the cupcakes. Scatter the frosted cupcakes with toppings and/or garnishes, if using.

For Bundt cakes: Brush the Bundt pan with softened unsalted butter and lightly coat with flour (or cocoa, for chocolate or mocha cakes). Prepare the batter as directed; pour into the prepared pan (the batter will fill the pan hallway to three-quarters full). Follow the baking times indicated in each recipe. Let the cake cool in the pan for 10 minutes, then invert it onto a wire rack. While the cake is still warm, use a skewer to pierce it all over at 1-inch intervals. Pour or brush the syrup over the cake. Set the cake aside to cool completely. (The syrup will soak into the cake.) When the cake is cool and no longer wet to the touch, about 1 hour, make the desired glaze according to the variation for Bundt glazes found at the end of each frosting recipe; use a spoon to drizzle the glaze over the cake. Scatter the glazed cake with toppings and/or garnishes, if using. Set the cake aside until the glaze sets, about 1 hour.

For 13 x 9-inch sheet cakes: Brush the 13 x 9-inch pan with softened unsalted butter and line with parchment paper or aluminum foil to overhang on the two longer sides by a few inches. Butter the parchment or foil, then dust it lightly with flour (or cocoa, for chocolate and mocha cakes). Prepare the batter as directed; pour into the prepared pan. Follow the baking time indicated in each recipe. While the cake is still warm, use a skewer to pierce it all over at 1-inch intervals. Pour or brush the syrup over the cake. Set the cake aside, in the pan, on a wire rack to cool completely. (The syrup will soak into the cake.) When the cake is cool and no longer wet to the touch, about 1 hour, make the frosting according to the variation for sheet cakes. Lift the cake from the pan using the overhang and transfer it to a serving platter. Frost the cake. Scatter the frosted cake with toppings and/or garnishes, if using.

SPLITTING A 2-LAYER CAKE INTO A 4-LAYER CAKE

Splitting cakes is best done with fully cooled cakes that have not yet been pierced and soaked with syrup. With the cake at eye level, insert a toothpick into the side halfway between the top and bottom of the cake. Rotate the cake a few inches and repeat; after a few turns you will have studded the side of your cake with toothpicks. Rest a serrated knife on top of the toothpicks, and use their placement as a guide as you saw inward toward the center of the cake. Turn the cake as you cut, following the guides and taking care to keep your knife level. Gently place your hand on top of the cake to keep the layer steady as you cut.

THE CAKES

THE CAKES IN THIS BOOK are as simple as it gets: based on an easy homemade mix and stirred together in one bowl with just a handful of additions. The Cake Magic! method makes baking a great cake possible for anyone. A quick review of some baking basics plus a few extra tips will make your next cake nothing short of unforgettable.

PAN PREP 101

THE CAKE RECIPES in this book were developed for 8-inch round, straight-sided pans made of uncoated aluminum. These pans are sometimes labeled "professional" pans. However, many other pans work well, too—as you can see from the pictures throughout—specifically, 9-inch round pans, 8- and 9-inch square pans, cupcake tins, Bundt pans, and 13 by 9-inch pans (metal only, please—stay away from glass here!). Note that changing the baking pan changes the cake's baking time, so I've outlined necessary time adjustments in each recipe. But because cake batters vary in density—a carrot cake batter is denser than a vanilla cake batter, for example—different cakes bake up differently. Your best bet is always to test for doneness: Crumbs should cling to a skewer or cake tester when it's inserted in the center of the cake.

A NOTE ABOUT BUTTERING AND FLOURING THE PANS

The basic cake recipes call for coating the pans with softened unsalted butter and lightly dusting them with flour (or unsweetened cocoa powder for the chocolate and mocha cakes) before adding the batter. This step seals the cakes as they bake, allowing them to slip out of the pans unscathed. While there are store-bought sprays and coatings that offer the same results, I prefer to stick with the classics.

When buttering the pan, use a pastry brush to apply room-temperature butter on the bottom and sides in an even coat. (Vegans: Swap non-hydrogenated vegetable shortening for the butter, as suggested in the variations.) This creates a nice layer for the flour to stick to and stays put, unlike melted butter, which tends to run. To dust the pan, add about a tablespoon of flour or unsweetened cocoa powder to the buttered pan, then swirl and turn the pan to coat the surface completely. Tap the pan firmly on your work surface so the excess flour jumps away from the sides and corners, then invert the pan to dump out the excess for a thin, even coating. (This step helps eliminate the possibility of a cake with a pasty white edge—the result of extra flour tucked into the corners of the pan.) Resist the urge to use either of the Cake Magic! baking mixes to dust the pan; they contain sugar, which encourages exactly what we're aiming to avoid: a sticky crust. Instead, I suggest keeping a small container of all-purpose flour next to your jar of baking mix and using it expressly for dusting the pans.

For the gluten-free cakes, I recommend using rice flour to dust the pan. It has a milder, less starchy flavor than the other gluten-free flours, and won't contribute any added texture to the cakes' outer edges.

For cupcakes, skip this buttering-and-flouring step in favor of the paper liners that make cupcakes so easy to transport and share. I always pick ones made of parchment or plain paper and take extra care to choose standard cups (about two inches in diameter) for my traditional tins.

MEASURING INGREDIENTS

WITHOUT GETTING TOO SCIENTIFIC, it's a good idea to remember that different ingredients have different volumes and densities, so it's important to use the right measuring cup for the right ingredient. A cup of flour and a cup of oil are very different things, and should be measured differently.

Liquids like oil should be measured in a liquid measuring cup—the kind often made of glass or plastic with units on the outside and a helpful spout—because it is specially designed to consider the volume of a liquid. Dry and solid ingredients, including flour and sugar but also peanut butter and yogurt, should be measured in dry measuring cups (usually sold in nested sets and thereafter forever in search of their mates). Since dry ingredients can settle in their packages, you should spoon them lightly into the measuring cup to aerate them to ensure an accurate measure. To finish the job, simply swipe the back of a butter knife or handle of a spoon across the top of the cup to knock off any excess.

MELTING CHOCOLATE

CHOCOLATE SHOULD BE MELTED GENTLY, using controlled low heat and frequent stirring. This can be achieved in two ways: on the stovetop or in the microwave. Regardless of your preference, the steps are the same: Heat the chocolate, stir it often, and remove it from the heat just before all of the chocolate is melted.

The stovetop method takes about five minutes, depending on the speed of your simmer and the amount of chocolate. Place the chocolate in a heatproof bowl and set it over a pan with a couple of inches of gently simmering water. Stir the chocolate often until it is almost completely melted. The microwave method is faster—it takes about two minutes—but it requires a more watchful eye to avoid scorching the chocolate. Place the chocolate in a microwave-safe bowl and microwave for about two minutes, or until the chocolate is almost melted. Using either method, the result should be smooth chocolate that is barely warm to the touch. (Before stirring it into a batter or frosting, it should feel neither cold nor hot to the touch; see page 134.) If it becomes crusty or no longer smells sweet, the chocolate has met a sad end by being overheated and, unfortunately, should be tossed. (In that case, consider making a vanilla cake instead—see page 144.)

MAKING SUBSTITUTIONS

THE RECIPES in this book are almost magical in their ease and flexibility. If you are in the mood to make a cake but don't have all of the supplies on hand, take heart—you may have another ingredient that can be swapped in.

These recipes call for full-fat, plain yogurt. If you don't have any around, an equal amount of either buttermilk or sour cream will work just as well. Strained yogurt, like Greek-style, is another decent substitute—just thin it first with a bit of milk or water to approximate the consistency of regular yogurt.

I like to use melted, unsalted butter for the rich flavor it lends to a homemade cake, but a mild oil can be used in its place if you're out of butter. The key is to pick a flavor-neutral oil, like canola or grapeseed. Oils like coconut or olive also yield similar results, but bear in mind that they offer their own distinct flavors.

Although you might understandably be interested in using whole-wheat flour or a sugar alternative in these recipes, I wouldn't recommend it. Whole-grain flours and alternative sweeteners have different basic characteristics than their more refined counterparts and will change the texture and balance of the cake.

MIXING IT UP

MIXING UP THE BATTERS couldn't be easier—they are all stirred together by hand. It's simple—so simple, in fact, that you might wonder if you missed a step. Here are a few pointers on stirring; it really requires even less effort than you might think.

Once you have your dry mix in the bowl, give it a quick stir with a whisk. Add any extra dry ingredients, then whisk again. Plop your wet ingredients on top, and using either the whisk or a wooden spoon, stir the wet into the dry. After a few rotations of your whisk or spoon, the batter will begin to swell slightly from the leavening—it shouldn't need much stirring after that. The goal is to blend the wet and dry ingredients into one smooth mixture with as little effort as possible (about ten stirs or fewer). A tender, delicious cake emerges from doing less, not more!

5 Tips for Baking a Perfect Cake

1   **Whisk the dry mix before measuring it;** it ensures each cup of mix has all of the ingredients it needs to work well.

2   **Use room-temperature ingredients:** They incorporate more thoroughly and bake more efficiently.

3   **For layers, divide the batter into two portions before pouring it into the pans:** Use a scale to weigh them to make sure they're equal (or measure the batter with a large liquid measuring cup and divide the results). It makes for even layers and even baking.

4   **After pouring the batter into the prepared pans,** quickly put them in the oven. If the batter sits out for more than a minute or two, it will lose some of its leavening power.

5   **Bake cakes on the center rack of the oven,** and resist the urge to open the oven door to check for doneness until five minutes shy of the suggested baking time.

TROUBLESHOOTING WONKY CAKES

BAKING A CAKE is filled with such good intentions that it can be terribly disappointing (and confusing) if it falls short. Here are a few common reasons and fixes for cakes that don't turn out as they should. If your cake is:

SUNKEN. The culprit is most likely the age of the leavening. An open container of baking powder, when stored in a cool, dry place, is effective for about 6 months. An open box of baking soda stored similarly also lasts only about 6 months. (The open box of baking soda stored in your fridge doesn't count—besides being of ambiguous age, it is also tainted with the various scents and smells from your fridge. Add a fresh box to your next grocery list.)

UNEVEN. A cake that varies in depth across its surface most likely has oven irregularities to blame. A cake rises because of the leavening, but *the way* it rises depends on the oven: its temperature, heat circulation, and orientation. The simple solution is to use an oven thermometer to ensure temperature accuracy. If the temperature is accurate but your cakes are still sloped, check to make sure the stove is level. (Follow the instructions for splitting cakes, page 122, to trim just the uneven top of the cake and no one will ever know.)

On the Level

There are myriad ways to level out uneven layer cakes. Some bakers trim off the domed tops, some invert the top layer onto the bottom so the domes kiss, some trim the domes off both layers and then invert the top layer... and so on. If I'm feeling especially formal, I might trim the top of my cakes to make the layers perfectly flat. But more often than not, I leave the layers as the oven made them and stack them bottom to top—no inversions or acrobatics necessary. The cakes will be delicious any which way.

EDGED IN WHITE. Cake layers that emerge from their pans coated in a white film are products of extreme pan preparation (see A Note About Buttering and Flouring, page 124).

BUBBLED ON TOP OR HOLEY. A cake with an irregular texture or appearance can signal an oven problem, but it can also result from a poorly mixed batter. If the ingredients aren't fully incorporated into the batter before baking, it can affect how the leavening reacts to the oven's heat. When stirring the batter, make sure to scoop from the bottom, and scrape down the side of the bowl as you go.

FREEZING "NAKED" BAKED CAKES

IF YOUR MOTTO IS "BE PREPARED," you may want to make cake layers ahead of time and freeze them. This is easy to do: Let the cake cool completely (skip the syruping step for now), wrap each layer separately in plastic wrap, then transfer each to its own resealable plastic freezer bag. Place each bag on a flat surface in the freezer until frozen solid (avoid stacking the layers on top of each other, if possible). To thaw the cake layers, remove the plastic bags and plastic wrap and place them on a wire rack at room temperature. They will thaw, depending on the temperature, in about two hours, and be ready for bathing in syrup (the cakes don't need to be warm in this case), assembling, and frosting.

Square layers and rectangular sheet cakes can be frozen in the same way as the round layers. Cupcakes should be frozen solid on a baking sheet before you transfer them to a resealable plastic freezer bag for storage.

Thawing instructions are the same as for the round cake layers. I don't recommend freezing Bundt cakes. Their shape makes them difficult to wrap well, and thus it's hard to preserve their texture and flavor once frozen.

THE SYRUPS

THERE ARE ONLY EIGHT BASIC CAKE RECIPES in this book, but all it takes is a quick flip through the chapters to see how each one can take on drastically different personalities—thanks largely to the use of flavoring syrups. These genius syrups are a professional baker's secret weapon: They guarantee a moist cake while adding subtle flavor to each bite. Each cake is treated as a canvas on which to layer flavors, and the syrups function as the first of them.

THE DEAL WITH THE SYRUPS

THE FORMULA FOR EVERY ONE of these game-changing syrups is the same: Combine the liquid ingredient with sugar, a pinch of salt, and, in most cases, an additional stir-in or two. The flavor possibilities are nearly endless, and what's more, the syrups can be made ahead (see page 131) to save time. Each of the recipes yields enough syrup to bathe any cake in the book, whether it's prepared as a layer cake, sheet cake, Bundt cake, or cupcakes.

The process is simple: After removing the hot cake layers from the oven, pierce them, still in their pans, at one-inch intervals with a skewer or a paring knife. This creates channels for the syrup to seep into the cakes. Then, pour or generously brush the syrup over the surface of the hot layers, dividing it between them as evenly as you can. Transfer the soaked layers (still in their pans) to a wire rack to cool completely. When they are cooled and are no longer wet to the touch, one to two hours, carefully turn them out of their pans and assemble and frost as directed (see page 120). (Note that cakes baked in a Bundt pan, sheet pan, or cupcake tins require different syruping techniques—see pages 121–122 for instructions.)

By bathing the cake layers in syrup right after they emerge from the oven, you make double use of the cooling time. While the layers cool, the syrup settles into the cake, changing the crumb and flavor with minimal work on the part of the baker.

HOW TO STORE THE SYRUPS

ALL OF THE FLAVORING SYRUPS can be made ahead of time. Simply let the syrup cool completely, transfer it to a tightly lidded glass jar or airtight container, then refrigerate for up to 1 week. Reheat it as directed to room temperature or warmer before using it to bathe the cake layers.

FROSTING + DECORATING

GREAT CAKES DON'T NEED FANCY DECORATIONS—there's no need to master piping rosettes or make the frosting smooth like draped satin. Instead, I encourage you to let the amazing flavors and textures of these cakes shine by keeping the decoration minimal. A few basic techniques will ensure beautiful results. Add a coating of, say, toasted coconut or a drizzling of homemade caramel and you'll have a cake that looks utterly delicious without being precious or intimidating. The aim is a cake that makes you want to grab a fork and dig in.

Each of the frosting recipes makes enough luscious frosting to coat one round or square 8-inch layer cake, a round 9-inch layer cake, or 24 cupcakes. For Bundt cakes, you may wish to use the proportions and method suggested for the sheet cake variations, or transform your chosen frosting into a glaze (I've given you directions on how to do this in the variations for each frosting recipe).

A NOTE ON SOFTENED BUTTER

YOU CAN TELL BUTTER IS PROPERLY SOFTENED when you can indent it easily with your thumb. The butter shouldn't look greasy or stick to its wrapping when you remove it. If it does, it's too soft and will make a droopy frosting that will need to be chilled before it is spread on the cake. Butter that's too hard won't combine well with sugar—a frosting fail. While the right consistency is key when it comes to butter, it's easy to achieve even if you didn't plan ahead.

The simplest way to soften butter takes time but little else: Place it on the counter away from heat or sun and forget about it for a while until it reaches room temperature. Alternatively, if you need to soften a stick or two in a hurry, an electric stand mixer fitted with the paddle attachment will do the trick. Cut the cold butter into pieces, place it in the bowl of the mixer, and beat on low speed. After some initial clunking, the butter will smooth out into a spreadable texture as it is kneaded and warmed. (Don't try this with a handheld mixer, however; it will burn out the motor.)

CREAMING BUTTER AND SUGAR

AMERICAN BUTTERCREAM FROSTINGS—the kind I play with in this book—stem from the basic action of whipping together butter and confectioners' sugar. I like cakes more than I do athletics, so creaming butter and sugar by hand is out of the question for me. A stand mixer fitted with the paddle attachment or a handheld electric mixer makes quick work of the task. All the baker has to do is recognize when the butter and sugar have been beaten and blended just the right amount.

To do that, combine the softened butter and sugar in the bowl of the electric mixer in two additions, and beat on low speed until the sugar is incorporated. From there, progress to medium speed and beat until the mixture is fluffy and pale and entirely free of sandiness from the sugar. It should plop from a spoon and spread easily. Once it does, voilà! You have frosting! Mix in any additional flavors and you're ready to go.

FROSTING FLAVORINGS

THE CAKE MAGIC! FROSTINGS span a wide array of flavors, though the recipes are very similar. While butter and confectioners' sugar are the common foundation, a variety of flavorings give each frosting a dramatically different personality. This combination of simplicity and versatility is echoed throughout all of the recipes in this book, making it possible to create big changes in flavor with only small adjustments.

For foolproof frosting, it is important to use each ingredient at the temperature specified, from room-temperature butter and cream cheese to cooled, melted chocolate. This is especially true for frosting flavorings: After taking the time to soften the butter and cream it with the sugar, adding hot flavorings, like freshly cooked caramel, can destroy your efforts. How to tell if a flavoring has cooled enough? Follow this simple rule: It should feel neither cold nor hot to the touch. (One exception: The caramels, pages 172 and 173, Caramelized Strawberry Jam, page 171, and Lemon Pudding, page 173, work well when added cold from the refrigerator.) In fact, the flavorings that start out hot are easily made ahead (and even doubled if you like—there's no such thing as too much caramel!). Once they've cooled, simply refrigerate them in an airtight container—they will keep for up to five days.

MAKE-AHEAD FROSTING TIPS

ALTHOUGH MAKING FROSTING IS SIMPLE, you can streamline your cake preparation even more by making it in advance. The finished frosting can be stored in the refrigerator in an airtight container for up to one week; simply let it sit out on the counter for a few hours before you plan to use it. You want it to be soft (but not greasy) so it spreads easily.

Frosting can also be frozen: Spoon it into resealable bags, squeeze out the excess air, then seal and label each bag with the frosting name and the date it was made. Wrap the bags in additional plastic and freeze. Once wrapped well and frozen, frosting can hang out in the freezer for up to 6 months. To return it to room temperature, thaw it overnight in the refrigerator, then set it out on the counter for a few hours until it is the same texture it was when it was freshly made.

Whichever storage method you use, make sure to stir the frosting vigorously or rewhip it with an electric mixer to restore its fluffy texture before using.

True Colors

I generally don't use food coloring to tint my frostings, but when the occasion calls for it (say, a special request from a soon to be four-year-old birthday boy), I opt for natural dyes. They yield lovely tints without the scary chemicals. My favorite is a "natural" trio by India Tree, which you can purchase at natural and specialty foods stores and also at Amazon.com. If you are adding food coloring, simply mix it into the finished frosting.

THE CRUMB-FREE CAKE

CRUMBS ARE THE ENEMY of a neatly frosted cake and can frustrate new bakers. There are two methods to combat stray crumbs. One is to spread a very thin—almost transparent—layer of frosting over the side and top of the cake. This base layer, once it has a chance to set, acts as a coating that seals in any wayward crumbs. It is known as a "crumb coat."

Crumb coats are useful for professional-style cakes, and can be pretty on their own (like in the Orange Mocha Cake with Cream Cheese Frosting on page 112), but my preferred method is a bit less fussy—it's more of a motion than a method. With a large glob—about ½ cup—of frosting on an offset spatula, spread the frosting in a fluid, wavy motion while moving the spatula forward. You can start on either the side or top of the cake, it's up to you. The important thing is to keep your spatula heaped with frosting as you frost new territory; you'll want to refill your spatula regularly and proceed along the side of the cake or from the outer edge of the cake toward the center. The hefty swipe of frosting keeps the spatula from coming into direct contact with the cake, which means it doesn't scrape up any crumbs, and the wavy motion coaxes the frosting onto the cake without pulling the frosting from the surface (and, with it, crumbs).

If you should happen to pull up some crumbs along the way, don't panic: There's an easy fix. First, clean your spatula. Then, use fresh frosting to pass over the area from another angle (being careful not to disturb the trouble spot). Lift away any rogue crumbs in the frosting with a clean spoon.

Now that you too hate crumbs, welcome to the club! Your cakes will be prettier than ever.

HOW TO MAKE A
SWIRLED FROSTING

A FEW OF THE CAKES IN THIS BOOK call for swirled or marbled frostings, in which a vibrant streak of something dreamy (usually caramel or a dessert spread, like cookie butter) peeks through the buttercream. It's easy to do, and it gives the cake that extra-decadent touch.

To make a swirled frosting, place the base frosting in a large bowl. Add a heaping spoonful of the swirl ingredient and loosely fold it into the frosting in one or two passes, just barely incorporating it (you should see subtle streaks of the swirl ingredient in the base frosting). As you spread this two-tone frosting on the cake, it will continue to marbleize. The secret to a successful marbled frosting is confidence: The less the frosting is stirred in the bowl and the fewer swipes used to spread it on the cake, the more dramatic the swirl will be.

HOW TO DUST A CAKE

THIS IS A PRETTY FOOLPROOF and low-stakes technique for dressing up a cake. Simply spoon ¼ cup of the powdery topping of your choice—say unsweetened cocoa powder or confectioners' sugar—into a fine-mesh sieve. Hold the sieve over the cake and gently tap the rim of the sieve with a teaspoon so that a small amount of powder falls through the mesh. Repeat to coat the cake as little or as much as desired.

HOW TO COAT THE SIDE OF A CAKE

FRESHLY FROSTED CAKES can be coated and/or topped with all sorts of ingredients—chocolate chips, shredded coconut, crushed pretzels, chopped toasted nuts, or rainbow sprinkles, to name but a few—for irresistible texture, flavor, and color.

After assembling and frosting the cake (see page 120), place about three cups of your desired coating in a bowl. With the freshly frosted cake still on its paper lining (to catch any fallen bits), grab a handful of the coating and, with your hand slightly flattened, gently press the coating onto the side of the cake. Work your way around the cake, pressing from the base of the cake toward the top, until the side of the cake is coated completely. If you want to coat the top as well, scatter a generous layer of the coating over the top of the cake (you can reuse what's fallen off the side, if need be), gently brushing off any excess. (Note: If using the toppings on a non-layer cake or cupcakes, you may have some left over. No matter—the toppings keep well and are delicious on ice cream!)

STORING FROSTED CAKE

ONCE FROSTED, the cake has a barrier that protects the layers from going stale, so it can be stored in a cake box, usually at room temperature, for a day without worry. (Cake boxes can be found at craft and bakery supply stores.) Once cut, however, the cake is best stored in an airtight container. The cut edges—the ones exposed to air—will dry out the cake, which is a shameful end to a beautiful homemade dessert. You can use a plastic container made for this purpose, or even just a cake box wrapped in plastic wrap.

Every baker I meet seems to have a strong opinion on whether to store frosted and assembled cakes in the refrigerator or at room temperature. I tend to agree either way—that is, how a cake should be stored is a question of environment. A baker knows the temperature of his or her house and I don't.

As a general rule, cakes are best stored at room temperature—that is, if the room is somewhere in the low 70s or below. The environment inside a refrigerator is very dry and can make a cake stale or crusty.

FREEZING LEFTOVER CAKE

In my house, leftover cake just doesn't happen. But, on the rare occasions when it does, I cut the cake into individual slices and freeze them. It's the ultimate solution for when you want to reward your future self.

To freeze slices of cake, line a sheet pan or large baking dish with waxed paper, freezer paper, parchment paper, or plastic wrap. Arrange the cake slices on the prepared pan so they don't overlap. Transfer the pan to the freezer and freeze until the slices are solid, about one hour. Remove the pan from the freezer and thoroughly wrap each frozen slice individually in plastic wrap. Transfer the wrapped slices to a resealable plastic freezer bag and freeze for up to three months. Thaw the unwrapped slices at room temperature for about thirty minutes before digging in.

The Extra-Somethings

Some of the cakes in this book call for additional garnishes, like a scattering of homemade Graham Cracker Crumble (page 179), a sprinkle of Rosemary Sugar (page 180), or a heap of Sautéed Apples (page 174). You can use these toppings and fillings as directed, skip them entirely (though I hope you won't!), or play around with them to create other combinations of your own. The options are limitless.

The Recipes

CAKE MAGIC! CAKE MIX

▼ **MAKES 4 CUPS** (ENOUGH FOR ONE 8- OR 9-INCH TWO-LAYER CAKE, ONE 13 x 9-INCH SHEET CAKE, ONE 10-INCH BUNDT CAKE, OR 24 CUPCAKES)

2½ cups all-purpose flour

1½ cups sugar

¾ teaspoon baking soda

¾ teaspoon baking powder

1 teaspoon table salt (see Note)

Place all of the ingredients in a large bowl and whisk together well to combine. Whisk the mix again before measuring.

NOTE: It's important to use table salt in the cake mix; other types will eventually settle out of the mix.

GLUTEN-FREE CAKE MAGIC! CAKE MIX

1 cup white rice flour (see Notes)

½ cup tapioca flour

⅓ cup coconut flour

⅔ cup millet flour

1½ cups sugar

1 teaspoon baking powder

1 teaspoon baking soda

1 teaspoon table salt (see Notes)

Place all of the ingredients in a large bowl and whisk together well to combine. Whisk the mix well before measuring.

NOTES: This blend of alternative flours has been chosen to mimic the qualities of all-purpose flour. It is a carefully calculated balance of protein, fat, and starch that makes a cake that is both soft and sturdy. If the flours are swapped or substituted, the result will change significantly. You can find individual flours on the shelves of national health-food retailers, such as Whole Foods, or online.

Be sure to use table salt here—other kinds will eventually settle out of the mix.

A Note on Prep, Storage + Big Batches

These mixes beg to be made ahead and kept on hand for whenever cake inspiration strikes. Make them in large batches and store them in a cool, dry pantry in an airtight container or resealable bag labeled with the date; they will keep for up to three months. When making a big batch, take extra care in whisking together the ingredients to ensure they're evenly incorporated—whisk them again just before you make your next cake, for good measure.

TO MAKE 8 CUPS MIX (ENOUGH FOR TWO CAKE MAGIC! CAKES):
Double the original recipe: 5 cups all-purpose flour + 3 cups sugar + 1½ teaspoons baking soda + 1½ teaspoons baking powder + 2 teaspoons table salt

TO MAKE 12 CUPS MIX (ENOUGH FOR THREE CAKE MAGIC! CAKES):
Triple the original recipe: 7½ cups all-purpose flour + 4½ cups sugar + 2¼ teaspoons baking soda + 2¼ teaspoons baking powder + 1 tablespoon table salt

VANILLA CAKE

MAKES ONE 8- OR 9-INCH TWO-LAYER CAKE (OR ONE 10-INCH BUNDT CAKE, ONE 13 x 9-INCH SHEET CAKE, OR 24 CUPCAKES)

Unsalted butter, at room temperature, for greasing the pans

All-purpose flour, for dusting the pans

4 cups dry Cake Magic! Cake Mix (page 142), whisked well before measuring

¾ cup full-fat plain yogurt (preferably not Greek yogurt, see page 126)

1 cup (2 sticks) unsalted butter, melted and cooled, or 1 cup vegetable oil

¾ cup water

2 teaspoons pure vanilla extract

4 large eggs, at room temperature

1 Preheat the oven to 350°F. Butter the bottom and side of the pan(s). Dust with flour to coat, then invert and tap out any excess. (If making cupcakes, use liners instead of greasing and coating the tins.)

2 Place the cake mix in a large bowl. Stir in the yogurt, butter, water, vanilla, and eggs until moistened and no lumps remain (be careful not to overmix). Divide the batter between the prepared pans.

3 Bake until the layers are domed and golden brown, and a few moist crumbs cling to a skewer inserted in the center of the cake, 35 to 40 minutes (40 to 50 minutes for a Bundt, 25 to 30 minutes for a 13 by 9-inch cake, and 20 to 25 minutes for cupcakes). (At this point, coat the layers with syrup as directed on page 130 and let them cool completely in the pans.)

VARIATIONS

Buttermilk Cake: Substitute buttermilk for the yogurt.

Vanilla Cinnamon Cake: Whisk 2 teaspoons ground cinnamon into the cake mix before adding the remaining ingredients.

Confetti Cake: Stir ½ cup rainbow sprinkles into the batter just before pouring it into the pans.

Pineapple Upside-Down Cake: Toss together 2 cups chopped fresh pineapple and ½ cup sugar in a small bowl. Divide the fruit mixture between the prepared pans, along with any accumulated juices. Prepare the batter and pour it over the fruit.

Vanilla–Olive Oil Cake: Substitute olive oil for the melted butter.

Gluten-Free Vanilla Cake: Dust the pan(s) with white rice flour. Use Gluten-Free Cake Magic! Cake Mix (page 143) for the cake mix.

Vegan Vanilla Cake: Grease the pan(s) with non-hydrogenated vegetable shortening and dust with flour. Whisk together the dry ingredients as directed. In a blender, combine 4 ounces firm tofu (crumbled and packed into ½ cup), 1½ cups water, 1 teaspoon cider vinegar or distilled white vinegar, 1 cup vegetable oil (instead of the melted butter), and vanilla. Blend until smooth and the texture of heavy cream, 30 seconds to 1 minute. (Omit the yogurt, eggs, and ¾ cup water.) Add the tofu mixture to the dry ingredients in Step 2 and proceed as directed.

DARKEST CHOCOLATE CAKE

MAKES ONE 8- OR 9-INCH TWO-LAYER CAKE (OR ONE 10-INCH BUNDT CAKE, ONE 13 x 9-INCH SHEET CAKE, OR 24 CUPCAKES)

Unsalted butter, at room temperature, for greasing the pans

½ cup sifted, unsweetened cocoa powder, plus extra for dusting the pans

4 cups dry Cake Magic! Cake Mix (page 142), whisked well before measuring

¼ teaspoon baking soda

4 ounces semisweet chocolate, melted (see page 125) and cooled

¾ cup full-fat plain yogurt (preferably not Greek yogurt, see page 126)

1 cup (2 sticks) unsalted butter, melted and cooled, or 1 cup vegetable oil

1 cup water

4 large eggs, at room temperature

1. Preheat the oven to 350°F. Butter the bottom and sides of the pan(s). Dust with cocoa powder to coat, then invert and gently tap out any excess. (If making cupcakes, use liners instead of greasing and coating the tins.)

2. Whisk together the ½ cup cocoa powder, cake mix, and baking soda in a large bowl to combine. Stir in the melted chocolate, yogurt, butter, water, and eggs until moistened and no lumps remain (be careful not to overmix). Divide the batter between the prepared pans.

3. Bake until the layers are domed and fragrant, and a few moist crumbs cling to a skewer inserted in the center of the cake, 35 to 40 minutes (40 to 50 minutes for a Bundt, 25 to 30 minutes for a 13 by 9-inch cake, and 20 to 25 minutes for cupcakes). (At this point, coat the layers with syrup as directed on page 130 and let them cool completely in the pans.)

VARIATIONS

 Cola Cake: Substitute cola (not diet) for the water.

 Gluten-Free Darkest Chocolate Cake: Dust the pan(s) with unsweetened cocoa powder. Use Gluten-Free Cake Magic! Cake Mix (page 143) for the cake mix and certified gluten-free semisweet chocolate, melted and cooled.

 Vegan Darkest Chocolate Cake: Grease the pan(s) with non-hydrogenated vegetable shortening and dust them with unsweetened cocoa powder. Whisk together the dry ingredients as directed. In a blender, combine 4 ounces firm tofu (crumbled and packed into ½ cup); 1½ cups water; 1 teaspoon cider vinegar or distilled white vinegar; 1 cup vegetable oil (instead of the melted butter); and 4 ounces dairy-free semisweet chocolate, melted and cooled. Blend until smooth and the texture of heavy cream, 30 seconds to 1 minute. (Omit the yogurt, eggs, and the 1 cup water.) Add the tofu mixture to the dry ingredients and proceed as directed.

LEMON CAKE

MAKES ONE 8- OR 9-INCH TWO-LAYER CAKE (OR ONE 10-INCH BUNDT CAKE, ONE 13 x 9-INCH SHEET CAKE, OR 24 CUPCAKES)

Unsalted butter, at room temperature,
    for greasing the pans

All-purpose flour, for dusting the pans

3½ cups dry Cake Magic! Cake Mix
    (page 142), whisked well before
    measuring

2 tablespoons finely grated fresh lemon
    zest

¼ teaspoon baking powder

¼ teaspoon baking soda

¾ cup whole milk

1 cup (2 sticks) unsalted butter, melted
    and cooled, or 1 cup vegetable oil

3 tablespoons freshly squeezed lemon
    juice

4 large eggs, at room temperature

1 Preheat the oven to 350°F. Butter the bottom and side of the pan(s). Dust with flour to coat, then invert and tap out any excess. (If making cupcakes, use liners instead of greasing and coating the tins.)

2 Whisk together the cake mix, lemon zest, baking powder, and baking soda in a large bowl. Stir in the milk, butter, lemon juice, and eggs until moistened and no lumps remain (be careful not to overmix). Divide the batter between the prepared pans.

3 Bake until the layers are evenly golden brown and a few moist crumbs cling to a skewer inserted in the center of the cake, 32 to 36 minutes (40 to 50 minutes for a Bundt, 25 to 35 minutes for a 13 by 9-inch cake, and 20 to 25 minutes for cupcakes). (At this point, coat the layers with syrup as directed on page 130 and let them cool completely in the pans.)

VARIATIONS

Grapefruit Cake: Substitute freshly squeezed grapefruit juice for the lemon juice and grapefruit zest for the lemon zest.

Lemon–Poppy Seed Cake: Add 1 tablespoon poppy seeds to the dry ingredients.

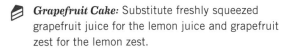

Lemon-Ricotta Cake: Substitute ½ cup whole-milk ricotta mixed with ¼ cup water for the ¾ cup whole milk.

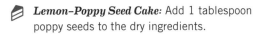

Lime Cake: Substitute freshly squeezed lime juice for the lemon juice and lime zest for the lemon zest.

Orange Cake: Substitute freshly squeezed orange juice for the lemon juice and orange zest for the lemon zest.

Gluten-Free Lemon Cake: Dust the pans with white rice flour. Use Gluten-Free Cake Magic! Cake Mix (page 143) for the cake mix.

Vegan Lemon Cake: Grease the pans with non-hydrogenated vegetable shortening and dust with flour. Whisk together the dry ingredients as directed. In a blender, combine 4 ounces firm tofu (crumbled and packed into ½ cup), 1½ cups water, 3 tablespoons freshly squeezed lemon juice, and 1 cup vegetable oil (instead of the melted butter), and blend until smooth. (Omit the eggs and milk.) Add the tofu mixture to the dry ingredients in Step 2 and proceed as directed.

BROWN SUGAR CAKE

MAKES ONE 8- OR 9-INCH TWO-LAYER CAKE (OR ONE 10-INCH BUNDT CAKE, ONE 13 x 9-INCH SHEET CAKE, OR 24 CUPCAKES)

Unsalted butter, at room temperature, for greasing the pans

All-purpose flour, for dusting the pans

4 cups dry Cake Magic! Cake Mix (page 142), whisked well before measuring

¼ teaspoon baking soda

⅓ cup packed light brown sugar

1 cup (2 sticks) unsalted butter, melted and cooled, or 1 cup vegetable oil

¾ cup full-fat plain yogurt (preferably not Greek yogurt, see page 126)

⅔ cup water

1 tablespoon unsulfured molasses

1 teaspoon pure vanilla extract

4 large eggs, at room temperature

1 Preheat the oven to 350°F. Butter the bottom and side of the pan(s). Dust with flour to coat, then invert and tap out any excess. (If making cupcakes, use liners instead of greasing and coating the tins.)

2 Whisk together the cake mix, baking soda, and brown sugar in a large bowl. Stir in the butter, yogurt, water, molasses, vanilla, and eggs until moistened and no lumps remain (be careful not to overmix). Divide the batter between the prepared pans.

3 Bake until the layers are domed and a few moist crumbs cling to a skewer inserted in the center of the cake, 40 to 45 minutes (40 to 50 minutes for a 10-inch Bundt, 25 to 35 minutes for a 13 by 9-inch cake, and 20 to 25 minutes for cupcakes). (At this point, coat the layers with syrup as directed on page 130 and let them cool completely in the pans.)

VARIATIONS

Brown Sugar–Cinnamon Cake: Add 1 teaspoon ground cinnamon to the dry mix.

Brown Sugar–Cinnamon Raisin Cake: Add 1 teaspoon ground cinnamon to the cake mix. Stir 1 cup raisins into the batter before dividing it between the prepared pans.

Brown Sugar–Nut Cake: Add 1 teaspoon ground cinnamon to the cake mix. Stir 1 cup chopped walnuts or pecans into the batter before dividing it.

Browned Butter Cake: Melt 1 cup (2 sticks) unsalted butter in a medium saucepan over medium heat. Let simmer and foam until speckled and golden brown, 6 to 8 minutes. Let the browned butter cool completely before substituting for melted butter in recipe.

Chocolate Chip Cookie Cake: Stir 1 cup semisweet chocolate chips into the batter before dividing it.

Root Beer Cake: Substitute root beer (not diet) for the water.

Gluten-Free Brown Sugar Cake: Dust the pans with white rice flour. Use Gluten-Free Cake Magic! Cake Mix (page 143) for the cake mix.

Vegan Brown Sugar Cake: Grease the pans with non-hydrogenated vegetable shortening and dust with flour. Whisk together the dry ingredients as directed. In a blender, combine 4 ounces firm tofu (crumbled and packed into ½ cup), 1½ cups water, 1 teaspoon cider vinegar or distilled white vinegar, and 1 cup vegetable oil (instead of the melted butter), and blend until smooth. (Omit the yogurt, eggs, and ⅔ cup water.) Add the tofu mixture to the dry ingredients in Step 2, and proceed as directed.

APPLE CAKE

MAKES ONE 8- OR 9-INCH TWO-LAYER CAKE (OR ONE 10-INCH BUNDT CAKE, ONE 13 x 9-INCH SHEET CAKE, OR 24 CUPCAKES)

Unsalted butter, at room temperature, for greasing the pans

All-purpose flour, for dusting the pans

4 cups dry Cake Magic! Cake Mix (page 142), whisked well before measuring

1 teaspoon baking powder

½ cup full-fat plain yogurt (preferably not Greek yogurt, see page 126)

1 cup (2 sticks) unsalted butter, melted and cooled, or 1 cup vegetable oil

¼ cup water

4 large eggs, at room temperature

3 cups peeled, coarsely grated apple

1 Preheat the oven to 350°F. Butter the bottom and side of the pan(s). Dust with flour to coat, then invert and tap out any excess. (If making cupcakes, use liners instead of greasing and coating the tins.)

2 Whisk together the cake mix and baking powder in a large bowl. Stir in the yogurt, butter, water, and eggs until moistened and no lumps remain (be careful not to overmix). Stir in the grated apple. Divide the batter between the prepared pans.

3 Bake until the layers are evenly golden on top and a few moist crumbs cling to a skewer inserted in the center of the cake, 40 to 45 minutes (40 to 50 minutes for a Bundt, 25 to 30 minutes for a 13 by 9-inch cake, and 25 to 30 minutes for cupcakes). (At this point, coat the layers with syrup as directed on page 130 and let them cool completely in the pans.)

VARIATIONS

Apple Cider Cake: Substitute unfiltered apple cider or apple juice for the water.

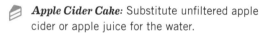 *Banana Cake:* Substitute 1 cup mashed banana (from 2 overripe bananas) for the apple.

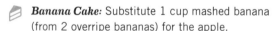 *Carrot Cake:* Substitute grated carrot for the apple.

Carrot-Lime Cake: Add 2 tablespoons freshly grated lime zest to the dry ingredients; substitute grated carrot for the apple.

Fresh Blueberry Cake: Substitute 1 cup pureed fresh blueberries for the apple.

Pear Cake: Substitute peeled and grated firm, ripe pear for the apple.

Pumpkin Cake: Stir 2 teaspoons ground cinnamon and 1 teaspoon ground nutmeg into the dry ingredients; substitute 1 cup canned pumpkin for the apple.

Zucchini Cake: Substitute grated zucchini for the apple.

Gluten-Free Apple Cake: Dust the pan(s) with white rice flour. Use Gluten-Free Cake Magic! Cake Mix (page 143) for the cake mix.

Vegan Apple Cake: Grease the pan(s) with non-hydrogenated vegetable shortening and dust with flour. Whisk together the dry ingredients as directed. In a blender, combine 4 ounces firm tofu (crumbled and packed into ½ cup), ¾ cup water, 1 teaspoon cider vinegar or distilled white vinegar, and 1 cup vegetable oil (instead of the melted butter), and blend until smooth and the texture of heavy cream, 30 seconds to 1 minute. (Omit the yogurt, eggs, and the ¼ cup water.) Add the tofu mixture to the dry ingredients in Step 2, add the apple, and proceed as directed.

PEANUT BUTTER CAKE

MAKES ONE 8- OR 9-INCH TWO-LAYER CAKE (OR ONE 10-INCH BUNDT CAKE, ONE 13 x 9-INCH SHEET CAKE, OR 24 CUPCAKES)

Unsalted butter, at room temperature, for greasing the pans

All-purpose flour, for dusting the pans

4 cups dry Cake Magic! Cake Mix (page 142), whisked well before measuring

¾ cup full-fat plain yogurt (preferably not Greek yogurt, see page 126)

½ cup smooth peanut butter

4 large eggs, at room temperature

1 cup (2 sticks) unsalted butter, melted and cooled, or 1 cup vegetable oil

1 cup water

1 Preheat the oven to 350°F. Butter the bottom and side of the pan(s). Dust with flour to coat, then invert and tap out any excess. (If making cupcakes, use liners instead of greasing and coating the tins.)

2 Place the cake mix in a large bowl. Whisk together the yogurt, peanut butter, and eggs in a small bowl. Add the peanut butter mixture, butter, and water to the cake mix and stir until moistened and no lumps remain (be careful not to overmix). Divide the batter between the prepared pans.

3 Bake until the layers are domed and a few moist crumbs cling to a skewer inserted in the center of the cake, 32 to 36 minutes (40 to 50 minutes for a Bundt, 25 to 35 minutes for a 13 by 9-inch cake, and 20 to 25 minutes for cupcakes). (At this point, coat the layers with syrup as directed on page 130 and let them cool completely in the pans.)

VARIATIONS

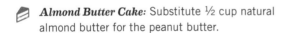 *Almond Butter Cake:* Substitute ½ cup natural almond butter for the peanut butter.

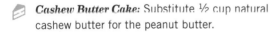 *Cashew Butter Cake:* Substitute ½ cup natural cashew butter for the peanut butter.

Pistachio Cake: Process 1 cup shelled unsalted pistachios in a food processor until they become a paste, about 5 minutes; substitute ½ cup of this pistachio butter for the peanut butter.

Spiced Almond Butter Cake: Add 1 teaspoon ground cinnamon to the cake mix; substitute ½ cup natural almond butter for the peanut butter.

Gluten-Free Peanut Butter Cake: Dust the pans with white rice flour. Use Cake Magic! Cake Mix (page 143) for the cake mix.

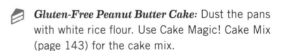 *Vegan Peanut Butter Cake:* Grease the pans with non-hydrogenated vegetable shortening and dust with flour. Whisk together the dry ingredients as directed. In a blender, combine 4 ounces firm tofu (crumbled and packed into ½ cup), 1½ cups water, ½ cup smooth peanut butter, 1 teaspoon cider vinegar or distilled white vinegar, and 1 cup vegetable oil (instead of the melted butter), and blend until smooth. (Omit the yogurt, eggs, and 1 cup water.) Add the tofu mixture to the dry ingredients in Step 2, and proceed as directed.

COCONUT CAKE

MAKES ONE 8- OR 9-INCH TWO-LAYER CAKE (OR ONE 10-INCH BUNDT CAKE, ONE 13 x 9-INCH SHEET CAKE, OR 24 CUPCAKES)

Unsalted butter, at room temperature, for greasing the pans

All-purpose flour, for dusting the pans

4 cups dry Cake Magic! Cake Mix (page 142), whisked well before measuring

¾ cup full-fat plain yogurt (preferably not Greek yogurt, see page 126)

⅔ cup melted and cooled unsalted butter or vegetable oil

¾ cup full-fat coconut milk

2 teaspoons pure coconut extract

4 large eggs, at room temperature

1 Preheat the oven to 350°F. Butter the bottom and side of the pan(s). Dust with flour to coat, then invert and tap out any excess. (If making cupcakes, use liners instead of greasing and coating the tins.)

2 Place the cake mix in a large bowl. Stir in the yogurt, butter, coconut milk, coconut extract, and eggs until moistened and no lumps remain (be careful not to overmix). Divide the batter between the prepared pans.

3 Bake until the layers are golden brown and a few moist crumbs cling to a skewer inserted in the center of the cake, 35 to 40 minutes (40 to 50 minutes for a Bundt, 25 to 30 minutes for a 13 by 9-inch cake, and 20 to 25 minutes for cupcakes). (At this point, coat the layers with syrup as directed on page 130 and let them cool completely in the pans.)

VARIATIONS

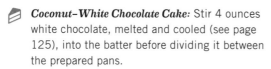

Coconut–White Chocolate Cake: Stir 4 ounces white chocolate, melted and cooled (see page 125), into the batter before dividing it between the prepared pans.

Coconut–Chocolate Chip Cake: Stir 1 cup semisweet chocolate chips into the batter before dividing it between the prepared pans.

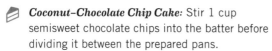

Spiced Coconut-Pecan Cake: Add 1½ teaspoons ground cinnamon and ½ teaspoon ground nutmeg to the dry ingredients; stir ½ cup unsweetened flaked or shredded coconut and 1 cup chopped pecans into the batter before dividing it between the prepared pans.

Gluten-Free Coconut Cake: Dust the pans with white rice flour. Use Gluten-Free Cake Magic! Cake Mix (page 143) for the cake mix.

Vegan Coconut Cake: Grease the pans with non-hydrogenated vegetable shortening and dust with flour. Whisk together the dry ingredients as directed. In a blender, combine 4 ounces firm tofu (crumbled and packed into ½ cup), 1½ cups full-fat coconut milk, 2 teaspoons coconut extract, 1 teaspoon cider vinegar or distilled white vinegar, and ⅔ cup vegetable oil (instead of the melted butter), and blend until smooth. (Omit the yogurt, coconut milk, and eggs.) Add the tofu mixture to the dry ingredients in Step 2, and proceed as directed.

MOCHA CAKE

MAKES ONE 8 OR 9-INCH TWO-LAYER CAKE (OR ONE 10-INCH BUNDT CAKE, ONE 13 x 9-INCH SHEET CAKE, OR 24 CUPCAKES)

Unsalted butter, at room temperature, for greasing the pans

½ cup sifted unsweetened cocoa powder, plus extra for dusting the pans

4 cups dry Cake Magic! Cake Mix (page 142), whisked well before measuring

¼ teaspoon baking soda

¾ cup full-fat plain yogurt (preferably not Greek yogurt, see page 126)

1 cup (2 sticks) unsalted butter, melted and cooled, or 1 cup vegetable oil

1 cup brewed espresso, cooled

4 large eggs, at room temperature

1 Preheat the oven to 350°F. Butter the bottom and side of the pan(s). Dust with cocoa powder to coat, then invert and tap out any excess. (If making cupcakes, use liners instead of greasing and coating the tins.)

2 Whisk together the ½ cup cocoa powder, cake mix, and baking soda in a large bowl. Stir in the yogurt, butter, espresso, and eggs until moistened and no lumps remain (be careful not to overmix). Divide the batter between the prepared pans.

3 Bake until the layers are domed and a few moist crumbs cling to a skewer inserted in the center of the cake, 32 to 36 minutes (40 to 45 minutes for a Bundt, 25 to 35 minutes for a 13 by 9-inch cake, and 20 to 25 minutes for cupcakes). (At this point, coat the layers with syrup as directed on page 130 and let them cool completely in the pans.)

VARIATIONS

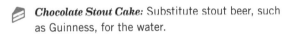 *Chocolate Stout Cake:* Substitute stout beer, such as Guinness, for the water.

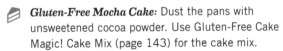 *Gluten-Free Mocha Cake:* Dust the pans with unsweetened cocoa powder. Use Gluten-Free Cake Magic! Cake Mix (page 143) for the cake mix.

Vegan Mocha Cake: Grease the pans with non-hydrogenated vegetable shortening and dust with unsweetened cocoa powder. Whisk together the dry ingredients as directed. In a blender, combine 4 ounces firm tofu (crumbled and packed into ½ cup), ½ cup water, the cooled espresso, 1 teaspoon cider vinegar or distilled white vinegar, and 1 cup vegetable oil (instead of the melted butter), and blend until smooth. (Omit the yogurt and eggs.) Add the tofu mixture to the dry ingredients in Step 2, and proceed as directed.

VANILLA SYRUP

GF • V MAKES 1 CUP

½ cup sugar

½ cup water

Pinch of salt

1 tablespoon pure vanilla extract, or the seeds scraped from 1 split vanilla bean

Combine the sugar, water, and salt in a small saucepan, bring to a boil over medium-high heat, and boil for about 5 minutes. Stir to dissolve the sugar, then stir in the vanilla and remove from the heat. Set aside to cool. Use the syrup warm or let it stand, covered, until it reaches room temperature.

Vanilla Syrup will keep, in an airtight container in the refrigerator, for up to 1 week. Reheat it in a small saucepan over low heat before using.

VARIATIONS

 Chocolate Syrup: Substitute ¼ cup unsweetened cocoa powder for the vanilla.

 Maple Syrup: Reduce the sugar to ⅓ cup and substitute ¼ cup maple syrup for the vanilla.

SWEET CREAM SYRUP

GF MAKES 1 CUP

½ cup sugar

½ cup heavy (whipping) cream

Pinch of salt

½ teaspoon pure vanilla extract

Combine the sugar, cream, and salt in a small saucepan and bring to a boil over medium-high heat. Stir to dissolve the sugar. Remove from the heat, stir in the vanilla, and set aside to cool. Use the syrup warm or let it stand, covered, until it reaches room temperature.

Sweet Cream Syrup will keep, in an airtight container in the refrigerator, for up to 1 week. Reheat it in a small saucepan over low heat before using.

VARIATIONS

 ***Milky Caramel Syrup:*** Stir ¼ cup Salted Caramel (page 172) into the Sweet Cream Syrup until combined.

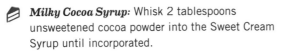 ***Milky Cocoa Syrup:*** Whisk 2 tablespoons unsweetened cocoa powder into the Sweet Cream Syrup until incorporated.

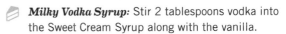 ***Milky Vodka Syrup:*** Stir 2 tablespoons vodka into the Sweet Cream Syrup along with the vanilla.

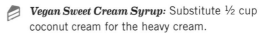 ***Vegan Sweet Cream Syrup:*** Substitute ½ cup coconut cream for the heavy cream.

MIXED BERRY SYRUP

GF • V MAKES 1 CUP

½ cup sugar

½ cup water

1 tablespoon seedless raspberry jam

1 tablespoon seedless strawberry jam

Pinch of salt

½ teaspoon pure vanilla extract

1 tablespoon cherry liqueur or Kirsch
(optional but recommended)

Combine the sugar, water, jams, and salt in a small saucepan and bring to a boil over medium-high heat. Stir to dissolve the sugar, then stir in the vanilla and liqueur, if using. Remove from the heat and set aside to steep, covered, for at least 20 minutes. Strain the syrup. Use the syrup warm or at room temperature.

Mixed Berry Syrup will keep, in an airtight container in the refrigerator, for up to 1 week. Reheat it in a small saucepan over low heat before using.

VARIATIONS

Blackberry Syrup: Substitute 2 tablespoons seedless blackberry jam for the raspberry and strawberry jams. Omit the cherry liqueur.

Blueberry Syrup: Substitute 2 tablespoons blueberry jam for the raspberry and strawberry jams. Omit the cherry liqueur.

Bourbon-Berry Syrup: Stir in 1 tablespoon bourbon with the vanilla and cherry liqueur.

Cherry Syrup: Substitute 2 tablespoons cherry preserves for the raspberry and strawberry jams.

Mango Syrup: Substitute ½ cup fresh or frozen chopped mango for the jams. Omit the cherry liqueur.

Peach Syrup: Substitute 2 tablespoons peach jam for the raspberry and strawberry jams. Omit the cherry liqueur.

Pear Syrup: Substitute ½ cup sliced fresh pears for the jams. Omit the cherry liqueur.

Raspberry Syrup: Substitute 1 tablespoon raspberry preserves for the strawberry jam; substitute 1 tablespoon Chambord for the cherry liqueur.

Strawberry Syrup: Substitute 1 tablespoon strawberry preserves for the raspberry jam. Omit the cherry liqueur.

RUM SYRUP

GF • V   MAKES 1 CUP

½ cup sugar

½ cup water

Pinch of salt

2 tablespoons dark or light rum

Combine the sugar, water, and salt in a small saucepan and bring to a boil over medium-high heat. Stir to dissolve the sugar, then stir in the rum. Remove from the heat and set aside to cool. Use the syrup warm or let it stand, covered, until it reaches room temperature.

Rum Syrup will keep, in an airtight container in the refrigerator, for up to 1 week. Reheat it in a small saucepan over low heat before using.

VARIATIONS

 *Amaretto Syrup:* Substitute amaretto for the rum.

Baileys Syrup: Substitute Baileys Original Irish Cream for the rum.

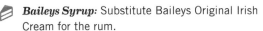 *Bourbon Syrup:* Substitute bourbon for the rum.

Buttered Rum or Scotch Syrup: Stir 1 tablespoon unsalted butter into the hot Rum or Scotch Syrup. Use warm.

 *Gingery Buttered Rum Syrup:* Add ¼ cup peeled, chopped fresh ginger to the saucepan with the sugar, water, and salt; prepare as directed. Stir 1 tablespoon unsalted butter into the hot syrup. Strain the ginger from the syrup before using. Use warm.

Scotch Syrup: Substitute Scotch for the rum.

COLA SYRUP

GF • *V* MAKES 1 CUP

½ cup sugar

½ cup cola (not diet)

Pinch of ground nutmeg

Pinch of salt

Combine the sugar, cola, nutmeg and salt in a small saucepan and bring to a boil over medium-high heat. Stir to dissolve the sugar. Remove from the heat and set aside to cool. Use the syrup warm or let it stand, covered, until it reaches room temperature.

Cola Syrup will keep, in an airtight container in the refrigerator, for up to 1 week. Reheat it in a small saucepan over low heat before using.

VARIATIONS

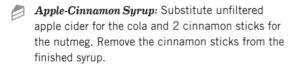 ***Apple-Cinnamon Syrup:*** Substitute unfiltered apple cider for the cola and 2 cinnamon sticks for the nutmeg. Remove the cinnamon sticks from the finished syrup.

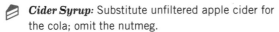 ***Cider Syrup:*** Substitute unfiltered apple cider for the cola; omit the nutmeg.

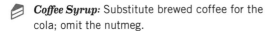 ***Coffee Syrup:*** Substitute brewed coffee for the cola; omit the nutmeg.

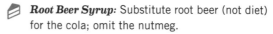 ***Root Beer Syrup:*** Substitute root beer (not diet) for the cola; omit the nutmeg.

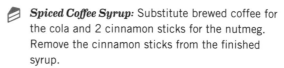 ***Spiced Coffee Syrup:*** Substitute brewed coffee for the cola and 2 cinnamon sticks for the nutmeg. Remove the cinnamon sticks from the finished syrup.

Stout Syrup: Substitute stout beer, such as Guinness, for the cola.

FRESH ROSEMARY SYRUP

GF • V MAKES 1 CUP

½ cup sugar

½ cup water

4 sprigs fresh rosemary

Pinch of salt

½ teaspoon pure vanilla extract

Combine the sugar, water, rosemary, and salt in a small saucepan and bring to a boil over medium-high heat. Stir to dissolve the sugar, then stir in the vanilla. Remove from the heat and set aside to steep, covered, for at least 20 minutes. Strain the rosemary from the finished syrup (if making Sugared Rosemary, below, reserve it). Use the syrup warm or at room temperature.

Fresh Rosemary Syrup will keep, in an airtight container in the refrigerator, for up to 1 week. Reheat it in a small saucepan over low heat before using.

VARIATIONS

 Fresh Basil Syrup: Substitute 4 fresh basil sprigs for the rosemary.

 Fresh Thyme Syrup: Substitute 6 to 8 fresh thyme sprigs for the rosemary.

Fresh Mint Syrup: Substitute 4 fresh mint sprigs for the rosemary.

Sugared Rosemary   MAKES 2 SUGARED ROSEMARY SPRIGS

To make Sugared Rosemary, use the rosemary strained from Fresh Rosemary Syrup. Remove two rosemary sprigs from the syrup after the sugar is dissolved; dredge in 2 tablespoons additional sugar to coat. Set aside to dry on waxed or parchment paper.

SPICED SYRUP

GF • V MAKES 1 CUP

½ cup sugar

½ cup water

2 cinnamon sticks

4 whole cloves

Pinch of ground nutmeg

Pinch of salt

½ teaspoon pure vanilla extract

Combine the sugar, water, cinnamon sticks, cloves, nutmeg, and salt in a small saucepan and bring to a boil over medium-high heat. Stir to dissolve the sugar, then stir in the vanilla. Remove from the heat and set aside to steep, covered, for at least 20 minutes. Strain the cinnamon sticks and cloves from the finished syrup. Use the syrup warm or at room temperature.

Spiced Syrup will keep, in an airtight container in the refrigerator, for up to 1 week. Reheat it in a small saucepan over low heat before using.

VARIATIONS

Apricot-Cardamom Syrup: Substitute 8 split cardamom pods for the cinnamon sticks, cloves, and nutmeg. Stir in 2 tablespoons apricot preserves with the vanilla. Strain the cardamom pods and apricot pieces from the finished syrup.

Cardamom Syrup: Substitute 8 split cardamom pods for the cinnamon sticks, cloves, and nutmeg. Strain the cardamom pods from the finished syrup.

Cinnamon Syrup: Use 4 cinnamon sticks instead of 2. Omit the cloves and nutmeg. Strain the cinnamon sticks from the finished syrup.

Cinnamon-Ginger Syrup: Use 4 cinnamon sticks instead of 2. Substitute ¼ cup chopped, peeled fresh ginger for the cloves and nutmeg. Strain the cinnamon sticks and ginger from the finished syrup.

Ginger Syrup: Substitute ¼ cup chopped, peeled fresh ginger for the cinnamon sticks, cloves, and nutmeg. Strain the ginger from the finished syrup.

Spiced Maple Syrup: Stir in 2 tablespoons pure maple syrup with the vanilla.

Spiced Red Wine Syrup: Substitute red wine for the water.

Sweet and Smoky Chile Syrup: Use 4 cinnamon sticks instead of 2. Substitute 2 whole dried chiles, such as chipotle, for the cloves and nutmeg. Strain the cinnamon sticks and chiles from the finished syrup.

TEA SYRUP

GF • V MAKES 1 CUP

½ cup sugar

½ cup water

Pinch of salt

2 tea bags (black tea)

Combine the sugar, water, and salt in a small saucepan and bring to a boil over medium-high heat. Stir to dissolve the sugar, then add the tea bags. Remove from the heat and set aside to steep, covered, for at least 20 minutes. Remove the tea bags from the finished syrup. Use the syrup warm or at room temperature.

Tea Syrup will keep, in an airtight container in the refrigerator, for up to 1 week. Reheat it in a small saucepan over low heat before using.

LIME SYRUP

GF • V MAKES 1 CUP

½ cup sugar

½ cup freshly squeezed lime juice

Pinch of salt

Combine the sugar, juice, and salt in a small saucepan and bring to a boil over medium-high heat. Stir to dissolve the sugar. Remove from the heat and set aside to cool. Use the syrup warm or let it stand, covered, until it reaches room temperature.

Lime Syrup will keep, in an airtight container in the refrigerator, for up to 1 week. Reheat it in a small saucepan over low heat before using.

VARIATIONS

 Lemon Syrup: Substitute freshly squeezed lemon juice for the lime juice.

 Orange Syrup: Substitute freshly squeezed orange juice for the lime juice.

COCONUT SYRUP

GF • V MAKES 1 CUP

½ cup sugar

½ cup full-fat coconut milk

¼ cup unsweetened shredded coconut

Pinch of salt

½ teaspoon pure coconut extract
(see Note)

Combine the sugar, coconut milk, shredded coconut, and salt in a small saucepan and bring to a boil over medium-high heat. Stir to dissolve the sugar. Remove from the heat, stir in the coconut extract, and set aside to steep, covered, for at least 20 minutes. Strain the coconut from the finished syrup. Use the syrup warm or at room temperature.

Coconut Syrup will keep, in an airtight container in the refrigerator, for up to 1 week. Reheat it in a small saucepan over low heat before using.

NOTE: Pure coconut extract is available in the spice aisle of most supermarkets.

BACON SYRUP

GF MAKES 1 CUP

4 slices uncooked bacon

½ cup sugar

½ cup water

½ teaspoon pure vanilla extract

Cook the bacon in a large skillet according to package directions. Transfer the bacon to paper towels to drain. Reserve 1 tablespoon bacon fat from the pan. Let the bacon cool, then crumble it.

Combine the sugar, water, and crumbled bacon in a small saucepan and bring to a boil over medium-high heat. Stir to dissolve the sugar, then add the vanilla and reserved bacon fat. Remove from the heat and set aside to steep, covered, for at least 20 minutes. Strain the bacon from the finished syrup (if making Candied Bacon, below, reserve the bacon). Use the syrup warm.

Bacon Syrup will keep, in an airtight container in the refrigerator, for up to 1 week. Reheat it in a small saucepan over low heat before using.

VARIATION

 Bacon-Maple Syrup: Stir in 2 tablespoons pure maple syrup with the vanilla.

Candied Bacon   MAKES ABOUT ¼ CUP

To make Candied Bacon, use the bacon strained from Bacon Syrup

1 **Preheat the oven to 350°F.** Line a large rimmed baking sheet with parchment paper.

2 **Pat the bacon dry** to remove any excess syrup, and arrange it on the prepared sheet.

3 **Bake until crispy,** about 10 minutes. Let cool completely before using. The cooled candied bacon pieces are best used right away, but will keep, in a resealable plastic bag or an airtight container at room temperature, for up to 3 days.

NUTELLA FROSTING

GF MAKES 4 CUPS

1½ cups (3 sticks) unsalted butter, at room temperature

½ cup Nutella or other chocolate-hazelnut spread, plus extra for swirling, if desired

Pinch of salt

4 cups (one 16-ounce box) confectioners' sugar

1 teaspoon pure vanilla extract

Combine the butter, Nutella, salt, and 2 cups of the sugar in a large bowl and beat with an electric mixer on low speed until incorporated, about 1 minute. Add the remaining sugar and beat on medium speed until the frosting is pale and no longer grainy, about 2 minutes. Add the vanilla and beat until the frosting is very light and fluffy, about 2 minutes.

Nutella Frosting will keep, in an airtight container in the refrigerator, for 1 week. Before using, bring it back to room temperature and stir it vigorously or beat it again for best results.

VARIATIONS

 Vegan Chocolate-Nut Frosting: Substitute 1½ cups non-hydrogenated vegetable shortening for the butter. Substitute ⅓ cup creamy peanut butter (or other nut butter) and 1 tablespoon unsweetened cocoa powder for the Nutella.

 Nutella Glaze for Bundt Cakes: Combine ¾ cup (1½ sticks) unsalted butter, ¼ cup Nutella, a pinch of salt, and 2 cups confectioners' sugar in a medium-size saucepan. Bring the mixture to a boil

and let boil, without stirring, 1 minute. Remove from the heat and stir in ½ teaspoon pure vanilla extract.

 Nutella Frosting for Sheet Cakes: Use ¾ cup (1½ sticks) unsalted butter, at room temperature; ¼ cup Nutella; a pinch of salt; 2 cups confectioners' sugar; and ½ teaspoon pure vanilla extract. Proceed as directed in the original recipe.

MALTED VANILLA FROSTING

MAKES 4 CUPS

1½ cups (3 sticks) unsalted butter, at room temperature

¾ cup malted milk powder

Pinch of salt

4 cups (one 16-ounce box) confectioners' sugar

2 tablespoons pure vanilla extract

Combine the butter, malted milk powder, salt, and 2 cups of the sugar in a large bowl and beat with an electric mixer on low speed until incorporated, about 1 minute. Add the remaining sugar and beat on medium speed until the frosting is pale and no longer grainy, about 2 minutes. Add the vanilla and beat until the frosting is very light and fluffy, about 2 minutes.

Malted Vanilla Frosting will keep, in an airtight container in the refrigerator, for 1 week. Before using, bring it back to room temperature and stir it vigorously or beat it again for best results.

VARIATIONS

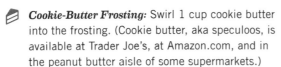

Cookie-Butter Frosting: Swirl 1 cup cookie butter into the frosting. (Cookie butter, aka speculoos, is available at Trader Joe's, at Amazon.com, and in the peanut butter aisle of some supermarkets.)

Gluten-Free Vanilla Frosting: Omit the malted milk powder.

Vegan Vanilla Frosting: Substitute 1½ cups non-hydrogenated vegetable shortening for the butter. Omit the malted milk powder.

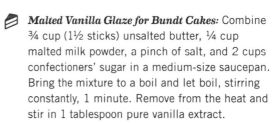

Malted Vanilla Glaze for Bundt Cakes: Combine ¾ cup (1½ sticks) unsalted butter, ¼ cup malted milk powder, a pinch of salt, and 2 cups confectioners' sugar in a medium-size saucepan. Bring the mixture to a boil and let boil, stirring constantly, 1 minute. Remove from the heat and stir in 1 tablespoon pure vanilla extract.

Malted Vanilla Frosting for Sheet Cakes: Use ¾ cup (1½ sticks) unsalted butter, at room temperature; ¼ cup malted milk powder; a pinch of salt; 2 cups confectioners' sugar; and 1 tablespoon pure vanilla extract. Proceed as directed in the original recipe.

CREAM CHEESE FROSTING

GF MAKES 4 CUPS

1 cup (2 sticks) unsalted butter, at room temperature

3 ounces cream cheese, at room temperature

Pinch of salt

4 cups (one 16-ounce box) confectioners' sugar

½ teaspoon pure vanilla extract

Combine the butter, cream cheese, salt, and 2 cups of the sugar in a large bowl and beat with an electric mixer on low speed until incorporated, about 1 minute. Add the remaining sugar and beat on medium speed until the frosting is pale and no longer grainy, about 2 minutes. Add the vanilla and beat until the frosting is very light and fluffy, about 2 minutes.

Cream Cheese Frosting will keep, in an airtight container in the refrigerator, for 1 week. Before using, bring it back to room temperature and stir it vigorously or beat it again for best results.

VARIATIONS

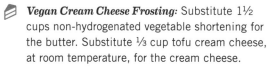 *Vegan Cream Cheese Frosting:* Substitute 1½ cups non-hydrogenated vegetable shortening for the butter. Substitute ⅓ cup tofu cream cheese, at room temperature, for the cream cheese.

Cream Cheese Glaze for Bundt Cakes: Combine ½ cup (1 stick) unsalted butter, a pinch of salt, and 2 cups confectioners' sugar in a medium-size saucepan. Bring the mixture to a boil and let boil, without stirring, 1 minute. Remove from the heat, add 1 ounce cubed room temperature cream cheese, and stir until combined.

Cream Cheese Frosting for Sheet Cakes: Use ½ cup (1 stick) unsalted butter, at room temperature; a pinch of salt; 2 cups confectioners' sugar; and 1 ounce cream cheese, at room temperature. Proceed as directed in the original recipe.

SALTED CARAMEL FROSTING

GF   MAKES 4 CUPS

1½ cups (3 sticks) unsalted butter, at room temperature

½ cup Salted Caramel (page 172), plus extra for swirling, if desired

½ teaspoon kosher salt

4 cups (one 16-ounce box confectioners' sugar

2 teaspoons pure vanilla extract

Combine the butter, caramel, salt, and 2 cups of the sugar in a large bowl and beat with an electric mixer on low speed until incorporated, about 1 minute. Add the remaining sugar and beat on medium speed until the frosting is pale and no longer grainy, about 2 minutes. Add the vanilla and beat until the frosting is very light and fluffy, about 2 minutes.

Salted Caramel Frosting will keep, in an airtight container in the refrigerator, for 1 week. Before using, bring it back to room temperature and stir it vigorously or beat it again for best results.

VARIATIONS

 Vegan Salted Caramel Frosting: Substitute 1½ cups non-hydrogenated vegetable shortening for the butter. Prepare and substitute Vegan Salted Caramel (page 172) for the Salted Caramel.

 Salted Caramel Glaze for Bundt Cakes: Combine ¾ cup (1½ sticks) unsalted butter, ¼ cup Salted Caramel (page 172), ¼ teaspoon kosher salt, and 2 cups confectioners' sugar in a medium-size saucepan. Bring the mixture to a boil and let boil, without stirring, 1 minute. Remove from the heat and stir in 1 teaspoon pure vanilla extract.

 Salted Caramel Frosting for Sheet Cakes: Use ¾ cup (1½ sticks) unsalted butter, at room temperature; ¼ cup Salted Caramel (page 172); ¼ teaspoon kosher salt; 2 cups confectioners' sugar; and 1 teaspoon pure vanilla extract. Proceed as directed in the original recipe.

BITTERSWEET CHOCOLATE FROSTING

MAKES 4 CUPS

1½ cups (3 sticks) unsalted butter, at room temperature

2 tablespoons unsweetened cocoa powder

Pinch of salt

4 cups (16-ounce box) confectioners' sugar

4 ounces unsweetened chocolate, melted and cooled (page 125)

Combine the butter, unsweetened cocoa powder, salt, and 2 cups of the sugar in a large bowl and beat with an electric mixer on low speed until incorporated, about 1 minute. Add the remaining sugar and beat on medium speed until the frosting is pale and no longer grainy, about 2 minutes. In a slow, steady stream, drizzle in the melted chocolate and beat until the frosting is very light and fluffy, about 2 minutes.

Bittersweet Chocolate Frosting will keep, in an airtight container in the refrigerator, for 1 week. Before using, bring it back to room temperature and stir it vigorously or beat it again for best results.

VARIATIONS

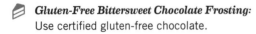 ***Gluten-Free Bittersweet Chocolate Frosting:*** Use certified gluten-free chocolate.

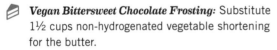 ***Vegan Bittersweet Chocolate Frosting:*** Substitute 1½ cups non-hydrogenated vegetable shortening for the butter.

Bittersweet Chocolate Glaze for Bundt Cakes: Combine ¾ cup (1½ sticks) unsalted butter, 1 tablespoon unsweetened cocoa powder, a pinch of salt, and 2 cups confectioners' sugar in a medium-size saucepan. Bring the mixture to a boil and let boil, without stirring, 1 minute. Remove from the heat, add 2 ounces chopped unsweetened chocolate, and stir until melted.

Bittersweet Chocolate Frosting for Sheet Cakes: Use ¾ cup (1½ sticks) unsalted butter, at room temperature; 1 tablespoon unsweetened cocoa powder; a pinch of salt; 2 cups confectioners' sugar; and 2 ounces unsweetened chocolate, melted and cooled. Proceed as directed in the original recipe.

LEMON PUDDING FROSTING

GF MAKES 4 CUPS

1½ cups (3 sticks) unsalted butter, at room temperature

½ cup Lemon Pudding (page 173; see Note)

Pinch of salt

4 cups (one 16-ounce box confectioners' sugar

Combine the butter, Lemon Pudding, salt, and 2 cups of the sugar in a large bowl and beat with an electric mixer on low speed until incorporated, about 1 minute. Add the remaining sugar and beat on medium speed until the frosting is very light and fluffy, about 4 minutes.

Lemon Pudding Frosting will keep, in an airtight container in the refrigerator, for 1 week. Before using, bring it back to room temperature and stir it vigorously or beat it again for best results.

NOTE: I urge you to make the Lemon Pudding on page 173 because it makes this frosting utterly irresistible, but if you're pressed for time or ingredients, feel free to use store-bought lemon curd in its place.

VARIATIONS

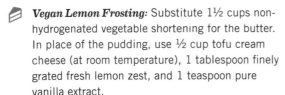 *Vegan Lemon Frosting:* Substitute 1½ cups non-hydrogenated vegetable shortening for the butter. In place of the pudding, use ½ cup tofu cream cheese (at room temperature), 1 tablespoon finely grated fresh lemon zest, and 1 teaspoon pure vanilla extract.

Lemon Pudding Glaze for Bundt Cakes: Combine ½ cup (1 stick) unsalted butter, a pinch of salt, and 2 cups confectioners' sugar in a medium-size saucepan. Bring the mixture to a boil and let boil, without stirring, 1 minute. Remove from the heat, stir in ¼ cup Lemon Pudding (page 173), and stir until combined.

Lemon Pudding Frosting for Sheet Cakes: Use ½ cup (1 stick) unsalted butter, at room temperature; a pinch of salt; 2 cups confectioners' sugar; and ¼ cup Lemon Pudding (page 173). Proceed as directed in the original recipe.

HONEY FROSTING

GF MAKES 4 CUPS

1½ cups (3 sticks) unsalted butter, at room temperature

½ cup Honey Caramel (page 173), plus extra for swirling, if desired

Pinch of salt

4 cups (one 16-ounce box) confectioners' sugar

1 teaspoon pure vanilla extract

Combine the butter, caramel, salt, and 2 cups of the sugar in a large bowl and beat with an electric mixer on low speed until incorporated, about 1 minute. Add the remaining sugar and beat on medium speed until the frosting is pale and no longer grainy, about 2 minutes. Add the vanilla and beat until the frosting is very light and fluffy, about 2 minutes.

Honey Frosting will keep, in an airtight container in the refrigerator, for 1 week. Before using, bring it back to room temperature and stir it vigorously or beat it again for best results.

VARIATIONS

Vegan Honey Frosting: Substitute 1½ cups non-hydrogenated vegetable shortening for the butter. Prepare and substitute Vegan Honey Caramel (page 173) for the Honey Caramel.

Honey Glaze for Bundt Cakes: Combine ¾ cup (1½ sticks) unsalted butter, ¼ cup Honey Caramel (page 173), a pinch of salt, and 2 cups confectioners' sugar in a medium-size saucepan. Bring the mixture to a boil and let boil, without stirring, 1 minute. Remove from the heat and stir in ½ teaspoon pure vanilla extract.

Honey Frosting for Sheet Cakes: Use ¾ cup (1½ sticks) unsalted butter, at room temperature; ¼ cup Honey Caramel (page 173); a pinch of salt; 2 cups confectioners' sugar; and ½ teaspoon pure vanilla extract. Proceed as directed in the original recipe.

MALTED MILK CHOCOLATE FROSTING

MAKES 4 CUPS

1½ cups (3 sticks) unsalted butter, at room temperature

¾ cup malted milk powder

Pinch of salt

4 cups (one 16-ounce box) confectioners' sugar

1 teaspoon pure vanilla extract

4 ounces semisweet chocolate, melted and cooled (see page 125)

Combine the butter, malted milk powder, salt, and 2 cups of the sugar in a large bowl and beat with an electric mixer on low speed until incorporated, about 1 minute. Add the remaining sugar and beat on medium speed until the frosting is pale and no longer grainy, about 2 minutes. Add the vanilla. In a slow, steady stream, drizzle in the chocolate and beat until the frosting is very light and fluffy, about 2 minutes.

Malted Milk Chocolate Frosting will keep, in an airtight container in the refrigerator, for 1 week. Before using, bring it back to room temperature and stir it vigorously or beat it again for best results.

VARIATIONS

 Gluten-Free Milk Chocolate Frosting: Omit the malted milk powder. Use certified gluten-free chocolate.

 Vegan Milk Chocolate Frosting: Substitute 1½ cups non-hydrogenated vegetable shortening for the butter. Omit the malted milk powder. Use dairy-free semisweet chocolate.

 Malted Milk Chocolate Glaze for Bundt Cakes: Combine ¾ cup (1½ sticks) unsalted butter, ¼ cup malted milk powder, a pinch of salt, and 2 cups confectioners' sugar in a medium-size saucepan. Bring the mixture to a boil and let boil, stirring constantly, 1 minute. Remove from the heat, add 2 ounces chopped semisweet chocolate (or ¼ cup chips), and stir until melted.

 Malted Milk Chocolate Frosting for Sheet Cakes: Use ¾ cup (1½ sticks) unsalted butter, at room temperature; ¼ cup malted milk powder; a pinch of salt; 2 cups confectioners' sugar; and 2 ounces semisweet chocolate, melted and cooled (see page 125). Proceed as directed in the original recipe.

STRAWBERRY FROSTING

GF **MAKES 4 CUPS**

1 cup (2 sticks) unsalted butter, at room temperature

3 ounces cream cheese, at room temperature

¼ cup Caramelized Strawberry Jam (page 171)

Pinch of salt

4 cups (one 16-ounce box) confectioners' sugar

½ teaspoon pure vanilla extract

Combine the butter, cream cheese, jam, salt, and 2 cups of the sugar in a large bowl and beat with an electric mixer on low speed until incorporated, about 1 minute. Add the remaining sugar and beat on medium speed until the frosting is pale and no longer grainy, about 2 minutes. Add the vanilla and beat until the frosting is very light and fluffy, about 2 minutes.

Strawberry Frosting will keep, in an airtight container in the refrigerator, for 1 week. Before using, bring it back to room temperature and stir it vigorously or beat it again for best results.

VARIATIONS

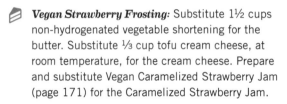 ***Vegan Strawberry Frosting:*** Substitute 1½ cups non-hydrogenated vegetable shortening for the butter. Substitute ⅓ cup tofu cream cheese, at room temperature, for the cream cheese. Prepare and substitute Vegan Caramelized Strawberry Jam (page 171) for the Caramelized Strawberry Jam.

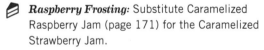 ***Raspberry Frosting:*** Substitute Caramelized Raspberry Jam (page 171) for the Caramelized Strawberry Jam.

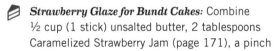 ***Strawberry Glaze for Bundt Cakes:*** Combine ½ cup (1 stick) unsalted butter, 2 tablespoons Caramelized Strawberry Jam (page 171), a pinch of salt, and 2 cups confectioners' sugar in a medium-size saucepan. Bring the mixture to a boil and let boil, without stirring, 1 minute. Remove from the heat and stir in 1 ounce cubed cream cheese, at room temperature, and ¼ teaspoon pure vanilla extract until combined.

Strawberry Frosting for Sheet Cakes: Use ½ cup (1 stick) unsalted butter, at room temperature; 2 tablespoons Caramelized Strawberry Jam (page 171); a pinch of salt; 2 cups confectioners' sugar; 1 ounce cream cheese, at room temperature; and ¼ teaspoon pure vanilla extract. Proceed as directed in the original recipe.

CARAMELIZED STRAWBERRY JAM

GF MAKES ½ CUP

½ cup seedless strawberry jam or preserves

2 tablespoons unsalted butter

Combine the jam and butter in a small saucepan and bring to a boil over medium-high heat. Boil, without stirring, 1 minute. Remove from the heat, stir occasionally, and let the jam cool completely before using (it will thicken significantly as it cools).

Caramelized Strawberry Jam will keep, in an airtight container in the refrigerator, for up to 2 weeks. Use chilled or at room temperature.

VARIATIONS

 Caramelized Raspberry Jam: Substitute seedless raspberry jam or preserves for the strawberry jam.

 Vegan Caramelized Strawberry Jam: Substitute coconut oil for the butter.

SALTED CARAMEL

GF MAKES 1 CUP

½ cup sugar

½ teaspoon kosher salt

2 tablespoons unsalted butter

2 tablespoons pure vanilla extract

½ cup heavy (whipping) cream

1 Combine the sugar and salt in a heavy medium-size saucepan over medium to medium-high heat. Cook, without stirring, until the sugar dissolves, about 2 minutes. Continue to cook, swirling the pan occasionally, until the caramel is deep amber and smells of toasted nuts but has not begun to smoke, 5 to 8 minutes.

2 Tilt the pan away from you and stir in the butter and vanilla. Add the heavy cream in a thin stream (the caramel will swell, bubble, and possibly splatter, so be careful and don't rush). Stir until the cream is incorporated, about 1 minute.

3 Remove the pan from the heat and let the caramel cool completely before using (it will thicken significantly as it cools).

Salted Caramel will keep in an airtight container in the refrigerator for up to 2 weeks. Use chilled.

VARIATION

 Vegan Salted Caramel: Substitute coconut oil for the butter and coconut cream for the heavy cream.

HONEY CARAMEL

GF MAKES 1 CUP

1 cup pure honey

3 tablespoons cold unsalted butter

Combine the honey and butter in a small saucepan and bring to a boil over medium-high heat. Boil, without stirring, 1 minute. Remove from the heat, stir occasionally, and let the caramel cool completely before using (it will thicken significantly as it cools).

Honey Caramel will keep, in an airtight container in the refrigerator, for 2 weeks. Use chilled.

VARIATION

 Vegan Honey Caramel: Substitute coconut oil for the butter.

LEMON PUDDING

GF MAKES 1 CUP

1 tablespoon finely grated lemon zest

½ cup sugar

2 tablespoons cornstarch

Pinch of salt

6 large egg yolks

½ cup freshly squeezed lemon juice (from about 6 lemons)

2 tablespoons cold unsalted butter

1 teaspoon pure vanilla extract

Combine the lemon zest, sugar, cornstarch, and salt in a medium-size saucepan. Whisk in the egg yolks and lemon juice until combined and cook, stirring constantly, over low to medium heat until the pudding is thick and velvety, about 10 minutes. Remove the pudding from the heat, then stir in the butter and vanilla until incorporated. Let the pudding cool completely before using (it will thicken significantly as it cools).

Lemon Pudding will keep, in an airtight container in the refrigerator, for up to 2 weeks. Use chilled or at room temperature.

SAUTÉED APPLES

GF MAKES 2 CUPS

2 tablespoons unsalted butter

2 large firm apples (1 pound), such as Gala, cored and sliced ½ inch thick

1 tablespoon sugar

Pinch of kosher salt

1 teaspoon freshly squeezed lemon juice

Heat the butter in a large skillet over medium-high heat until melted and foaming, about 1 minute. Add the apples in a single layer and sprinkle with the sugar and salt. Cook, stirring gently once, until the apples have softened slightly and become golden brown at the edges, about 3 minutes. Add the lemon juice and toss gently to coat. Let cool completely before using.

VARIATION

 Sautéed Pears: Substitute firm pears, such as Bosc, for the apples.

To Peel or Not to Peel?

A number of the cakes call for sliced fruit as a filling or a topping—sometimes both. While you may wish to peel certain fruits before slicing them, I usually don't bother. It's your call!

To peel firm or thick-skinned fruits, like apples, simply use a swivel vegetable peeler. For more delicate stone fruit, like peaches, you'll want to blanch them first:

Cut a small X in the bottom of each peach. Drop the peaches into a large pot of boiling water for 30 seconds. Use a slotted spoon to transfer the peaches to an ice bath; let them sit for 30 seconds, then peel off the skins with your fingers.

CARAMELIZED BANANAS

GF MAKES 1 CUP

1 large banana (about 8 ounces), peeled, halved crosswise, and sliced lengthwise (to make 4 pieces)

1 tablespoon melted butter

1 tablespoon sugar

1 Preheat the broiler with a rack in the highest position.

2 Arrange the banana pieces, cut-side up, in a broiler-proof dish or pan. Brush the cut sides of the banana with the butter and sprinkle with the sugar. Broil, watching carefully to avoid burning, until the bananas are browned and bubbly, 2 to 5 minutes. Let cool completely before using.

VARIATIONS

 Caramelized Mango: In place of the banana, use 1 mango, peeled, pitted, and cut into strips. Arrange the mango in a broiler-proof dish, brush with the butter and sprinkle with the sugar. Proceed as directed.

 Roasted Grapes: Brush 1 large bunch seedless red or green grapes (about ¾ pound) with the melted butter and sprinkle with the sugar. Transfer to a broiler-proof dish and proceed as directed.

 Caramelized Grapefruit: Use 1 large grapefruit, peeled and sliced crosswise into rounds, in place of the banana.

TOASTED COCONUT

GF • V MAKES 2 CUPS

2 cups sweetened or unsweetened flaked or shredded coconut

1 Preheat the oven to 350°F. Line a large rimmed baking sheet with parchment paper.

2 Scatter the coconut in a thin layer on the prepared baking sheet and bake until lightly golden around the edges, about 5 minutes. Use a spatula to turn and toss the coconut on the pan and expose the untoasted pieces. Return the pan to the oven and continue to bake, tossing the coconut regularly (watch it closely—it can burn easily), until intensely fragrant and golden brown, about 5 minutes more. Let cool on the baking sheet.

Toasted Coconut will keep, in an airtight container at room temperature, for up to 1 month.

VARIATION

 Toasted Nuts: Substitute chopped or whole pecans, pistachios, hazelnuts, almonds, walnuts, or whole pine nuts for the coconut and bake until fragrant and a shade darker, 8 to 12 minutes, depending on the type and size.

TOASTED MARSHMALLOWS

MAKES 2 CUPS

2 cups miniature marshmallows

1 Line a large rimmed baking sheet with parchment paper. Scatter the marshmallows on the prepared baking sheet and freeze until solid, about 10 minutes.

2 Heat the broiler with the broiler rack in the highest position. Broil the marshmallows, shaking the pan occasionally, until evenly golden brown and charred in spots, 1 to 2 minutes. Remove the marshmallows from the pan with a thin metal spatula. Use immediately.

WALNUTS IN SYRUP

GF MAKES 1 CUP

1 cup walnuts, roughly chopped, toasted if desired (page 176)

½ cup pure maple syrup

½ cup light agave nectar

Pinch of ground cinnamon

Pinch of salt

4 tablespoons (½ stick) cold unsalted butter

Combine the walnuts, maple syrup, agave, cinnamon, salt, and butter in a medium-size saucepan and bring to a boil over medium-high heat. Boil, without stirring, until the walnuts have softened and the syrup has thickened slightly, about 1 minute. Let cool completely before using (the mixture will thicken as it cools).

Walnuts in Syrup will keep, in an airtight container in the refrigerator, for up to 2 weeks. Let it come to room temperature before using.

VARIATIONS

 Hazelnuts in Syrup: Substitute hazelnuts for the walnuts.

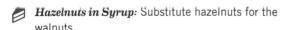 ***Pecans in Syrup:*** Substitute pecan pieces for the walnuts.

 Vegan Walnuts in Syrup: Substitute coconut oil for the butter.

BITTERSWEET CHOCOLATE GLAZE

MAKES 1 CUP

½ cup heavy (whipping) cream

2 tablespoons light agave nectar

Pinch of salt

4 ounces bittersweet chocolate, chopped

1 Combine the cream, agave, and salt in a heavy, medium-size saucepan over medium to medium-high heat. Bring to a boil and let boil, without stirring, 1 minute.

2 Remove the pan from the heat and add the chocolate. Let stand for 5 minutes, swirling the pan occasionally. Stir until the chocolate has melted and the sauce is thick.

3 Let cool completely before pouring over a frosted cake for decoration.

Bittersweet Chocolate Glaze will keep, in an airtight container in the refrigerator, for up to 2 weeks. When ready to use, reheat it gently in a heatproof bowl in the microwave, stirring often, until the glaze is loosened and just warm to the touch, about 3 minutes.

VARIATIONS

 Gluten-Free Bittersweet Chocolate Glaze: Use certified gluten-free bittersweet chocolate.

 Vegan Bittersweet Chocolate Glaze: Substitute ½ cup coconut cream for the heavy cream and use dairy-free bittersweet chocolate.

How to Shave Chocolate

Chocolate is a helpful ingredient to keep on hand for an easy last-minute garnish. To make chocolate curls, heat a piece of chocolate with a 1- to 2-inch-wide surface in the microwave at a reduced power setting until very slightly softened, a few seconds. Remove from the microwave and draw a swivel vegetable peeler across the surface of the chocolate. To make more rustic curls that shatter as they are tightly wound, heat a flat bar of chocolate the same way and draw a sharp knife across the bar's widest and smoothest surface. Alternatively, use a Microplane to grate room-temperature chocolate directly over the cake for a powdery look.

GRAHAM CRACKER CRUMBLE

MAKES ABOUT 3 CUPS

2 sleeves graham crackers (about
   10 cracker sheets), finely crushed
   (about 2 cups)

¼ cup malted milk powder

2 tablespoons sugar

½ teaspoon kosher salt

6 tablespoons (¾ stick) unsalted
   butter, melted

1 Preheat the oven to 300°F. Line a large rimmed baking sheet
with parchment paper.

2 Combine the graham cracker crumbs, malted milk powder,
sugar, and salt in a large bowl and toss to combine. Drizzle the
melted butter over the crumb mixture and stir until clumps
form.

3 Scatter the clumps onto the prepared baking sheet in a single
layer. Bake until the crumbles are golden brown and fragrant,
10 to 15 minutes. Let cool completely before using.

Graham Cracker Crumble will keep, in an airtight container at
room temperature, for up to 3 days.

VARIATIONS

 Chocolate Cookie Crumble: Substitute 2 cups
crushed chocolate wafers for the graham cracker
crumbs.

 Gingersnap Crumble: Substitute 2 cups crushed
gingersnaps for the graham cracker crumbs.

 Ladyfinger Crumble: Substitute 2 cups crushed
ladyfingers for the graham cracker crumbs.

 Oat Streusel: Place 1½ cups rolled oats in a food
processor and pulse to the texture of coarse meal.
Substitute ground oats for the graham cracker
crumbs.

 Shortbread Crumble: Substitute 2 cups crushed
shortbread cookies for the graham cracker crumbs.

CINNAMON SUGAR

GF • V MAKES ABOUT ½ CUP

½ cup confectioners' sugar

2 tablespoons ground cinnamon

Whisk together the sugar and cinnamon in a small bowl. Transfer the mixture to a fine-mesh sieve for dusting on cakes.

Cinnamon Sugar can be made in advance: it will keep, in an airtight container at room temperature, for up to 1 month. Whisk it before using.

VARIATION

 Spiced Chocolate Sugar: Add 2 tablespoons unsweetened cocoa powder to the cinnamon sugar mixture.

BASIL SUGAR

GF • V MAKES 1 CUP

1 cup white sanding sugar (see Note)

¼ cup chopped fresh basil leaves

Pinch of salt

Combine all of the ingredients in a food processor. Pulse until the sugar is green and sandy.

Basil Sugar will keep, in an airtight container at room temperature, for up to 3 days.

NOTE: Sanding sugar is granulated sugar with coarse crystals. It is available in the baking aisle of some supermarkets, at major cookware retailers like Williams-Sonoma, and online.

VARIATIONS

 Crystallized Ginger Sugar: Substitute ¼ cup crystallized ginger for the herbs.

 Rosemary Sugar: Substitute ¼ cup whole fresh rosemary leaves for the basil.

 Sandy Cinnamon Sugar: Substitute 1 chopped cinnamon stick for the basil.

 Thyme Sugar: Substitute ¼ cup whole fresh thyme leaves for the basil.

HOMEMADE VANILLA EXTRACT

GF • V MAKES 2 CUPS

8 vanilla beans (see Notes)

About 2 cups vodka or bourbon (see Notes)

Using the sharp tip of a paring knife, slice the vanilla beans in half lengthwise. Place the vanilla bean halves in a glass jar or bottle with a 3-cup capacity; add enough of the vodka to cover the pods. Cover and let infuse in a cool, dry place for at least 3 months before using.

NOTES: In terms of provenance, vanilla beans are as meticulously sourced and curated as the beans you'd find in a Brooklyn coffee shop. Vanilla beans hail from a wide range of tropical climates, each boasting different pod characteristics. For the purposes of homemade vanilla extract, Grade B vanilla beans—which are slightly imperfect-looking and thus cheaper—are perfect.

Homemade vanilla extract is yet another baker's secret to making your from-scratch cakes taste truly outstanding. Making it at home not only is easy and yields a lot, but it also gives you another chance to customize flavors. Use vodka, as written in this recipe, to allow the vanilla to sing clearly, or use bourbon for a smokier note.

CONVERSION TABLES

APPROXIMATE EQUIVALENTS

1 stick butter	8 tbs / 4 oz / ½ cup
1 cup all-purpose presifted flour or dried bread crumbs	5 oz
1 cup granulated sugar	8 oz
1 cup (packed) brown sugar	6 oz
1 cup confectioners' sugar	4½ oz
1 cup honey or syrup	12 oz
1 cup grated cheese	4 oz
1 cup dried beans	6 oz
1 large egg	about 2 oz or about 3 tbs
1 egg yolk	about 1 tbs
1 egg white	about 2 tbs

Please note that all conversions are approximate but close enough to be useful when converting from one system to another.

WEIGHT CONVERSION

US/UK	Metric	US/UK	Metric
½ oz	15 g	7 oz	200 g
1 oz	30 g	8 oz	250 g
1½ oz	45 g	9 oz	275 g
2 oz	60 g	10 oz	300 g
2½ oz	75 g	11 oz	325 g
3 oz	90 g	12 oz	350 g
3½ oz	100 g	13 oz	375 g
4 oz	125 g	14 oz	400 g
5 oz	150 g	15 oz	450 g
6 oz	175 g	1 lb	500 g

LIQUID CONVERSION

US	Imperial	Metric
2 tbs	1 fl oz	30 ml
3 tbs	1½ fl oz	45 ml
¼ cup	2 fl oz	60 ml
⅓ cup	2½ fl oz	75 ml
⅓ cup + *1 tbs*	3 fl oz	90 ml
⅓ cup + *2 tbs*	3½ fl oz	100 ml
½ cup	4 fl oz	125 ml
⅔ cup	5 fl oz	150 ml
¾ cup	6 fl oz	175 ml
¾ cup + *2 tbs*	7 fl oz	200 ml
1 cup	8 fl oz	250 ml
1 cup + *2 tbs*	9 fl oz	275 ml
1¼ cups	10 fl oz	300 ml
1⅓ cups	11 fl oz	325 ml
1½ cups	12 fl oz	350 ml
1⅔ cups	13 fl oz	375 ml
1¾ cups	14 fl oz	400 ml
1¾ cups + *2 tbs*	15 fl oz	450 ml
2 cups (*1 pint*)	16 fl oz	500 ml
2½ cups	20 fl oz (*1 pint*)	600 ml
3¾ cups	1½ pints	900 ml
4 cups	1¾ pints	1 liter

OVEN TEMPERATURES

°F	Gas Mark	°C	°F	Gas Mark	°C
250	½	120	400	6	200
275	1	140	425	7	220
300	2	150	450	8	230
325	3	160	475	9	240
350	4	180	500	10	260
375	5	190			

Note: Reduce the temperature by 20°C (68°F) for fan-assisted ovens.

INDEX

Pumpkin:
  cake, 148
  -chocolate cake, 73, *73*
  -ginger cake with cream cheese
    frosting, 75, *75*

R
Raisin cinnamon–brown sugar
    cake, 147
Raspberry:
  frosting, 170
  jam, caramelized, 171
  syrup, 154
Roasted grapes, 175
Root beer:
  cake, 147
  float cake, 60, *60*
  syrup, 156
Rosemary:
  sugar, 180
  sugared, 157
  syrup, fresh, 157
Rum:
  raisin cake, 61, *61*
  syrup, 155

S
Salted caramel, 172
Salted caramel chocolate cake, 30, *30*
Salted caramel frosting, 165
Sandy cinnamon sugar, 180
Sautéed apples, 174
Sautéed pears, 174
School lunch cake, 84, *84*
Scotch syrup, 155
Sheet cakes, adapting recipes for,
    121–22
Shortbread crumble, 179
S'mores cake, 58, *58*
Soda fountain cake, 35, *35*
Southern diner cake, 54, *54*
Speculoos:
  cookie-butter cake, 55, *55*
  cookie-butter frosting, 163
Spiced:
  almond butter cake, 149
  almond cake with cream cheese

frosting, 93, *93*
chocolate sugar, 180
coconut-pecan cake, 150
coffee + cream cake, 116, *116*
coffee syrup, 156
grapefruit + cream cake,
    46, *46*
maple syrup, 158
red wine syrup, 158
syrup, 158
Spicy cinnamon cake with apples,
    18, *18*
Spicy hot chocolate cake, 36, *36*
Stout syrup, 156
Strawberry:
  frosting, 170
  jam, caramelized, 171
  -lemon cake, 43, *43*
  syrup, 154
Sugar:
  basil; variations, 180
  cinnamon; variation, 180
  see also Brown sugar
Sugared rosemary, 157
Summer lemon cake, 40, *40*
Sweet and smoky chile syrup,
    158
Sweet cream cake, 7, *7*
Sweet cream syrup, 153
Syrups (+ variations):
  about, 130–31
  bacon, 161
  coconut, 160
  cola, 156
  fresh rosemary, 157
  lime, 159
  mixed berry, 154
  rum, 155
  spiced, 158
  storing, 131
  sweet cream, 153
  tea, 159
  vanilla, 152

T
Tea syrup, 159
Tea with cream + sugar cake, 67, *67*

Thyme:
  sugar, 180
  syrup, fresh, 157
Tiramisu cake, 115, *115*
Toasted coconut, 176
Toasted marshmallows, 177
Toasted nuts, 176
Toffee cake, 66, *66*
Toppings, note about, 139
Triple citrus cake, 47, *47*

V
Vanilla:
  cake, 144
  cakes, list of, 5
  cherry + chocolate cake, 10, *10*
  -cinnamon cake, 144
  extract, homemade, 181
  –olive oil cake, 144
  –olive oil cake with rosemary +
    lemon, 20, *20*
  syrup, 152
Vegan recipes, note about, 3
Vegetables:
  list of cakes with, 69
  see also specific vegetables
Vodka:
  homemade vanilla extract,
    181
  syrup, milky, 153

W
Walnuts:
  brown sugar–nut cake, 147
  in syrup, 177
Warm chocolate gingerbread cake,
    25, *25*
White chocolate–coconut cake,
    150
White Russian cake, 19, *19*
Wine, red, syrup, spiced, 158

Z
Zucchini:
  cake, 148
  -thyme cake with lemon pudding
    frosting, 74, *74*